FAMILY COOKING

Edited by
Jean Prince

Contents

This edition first published 1980 by
Octopus Books Limited,
59 Grosvenor Street, London W.1.

© 1980 Octopus Books Limited

ISBN 0 7064 1342 3

Produced and printed in Hong Kong by
Mandarin Publishers Limited,
22a Westlands Road, Quarry Bay,
Hong Kong

Cover photography by Paul Williams

Frontispiece: VEAL PAPRIKA *(page 42) (Photograph: Stork Advisory Bureau)*

Weights and Measures

All measurements in this book are given in Metric, Imperial and American.

Measurements in weight in the Imperial and American system are the same. Liquid measurements are different, and the following table shows the equivalents:

Liquid measurements
1 Imperial pint .... 20 fluid ounces
1 American pint...................................... 16 fluid ounces
1 American cup .... 8 fluid ounces

Level spoon measurements
1 tablespoon .... 15 ml
1 teaspoon .... 5 ml

Remember that the ingredients columns are not interchangeable. Follow only one set of measures.

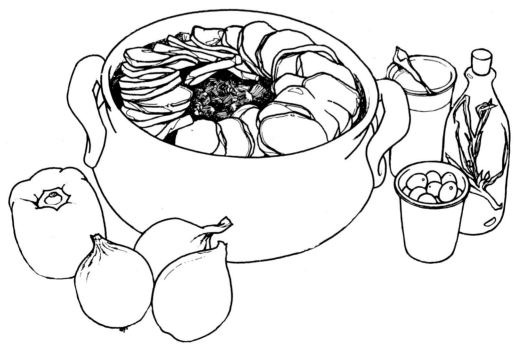

INTRODUCTION

There is nothing more appetizing than the smell of home-made soups, of simmering casseroles and freshly baked pies. And in these days when convenience foods proliferate, more and more people are returning to the kitchen to produce good, wholesome home cooking.

If you, too, would like to rediscover those delicious aromas, but are lost for ideas, just turn the pages of this book and you will find lots of tempting recipes that will bring a flow of compliments from your family.

You will find also that producing good nutritious meals – using fresh foods that provide all the vitamins and nutrients for a healthy way of life – does not mean spending hours in the kitchen. These specially chosen recipes are tasty, nutritious *and* easy to prepare. And many are illustrated in full colour to provide you with inspiration for the garnish and attractive presentation that transforms everyday cooking into something special.

Whatever your taste, whatever your budget, you will find plenty of recipes that you will want to cook time and time again.

There are tasty cold soups, hot soups, nourishing meal-in-a-bowl soups. There is a good choice of main meal dishes, including old family standbys like Chilli (Chili) con Carne and new recipes that won't stretch your budget, such as Gruyère Soufflé, plus a selection of vegetable dishes to add variety and colour to your weekly menus. Salads, too, are important to a well balanced diet and I have included recipes to prove that there is much more to a salad than a few limp lettuce leaves and wedges of cucumber and tomato! They all take very little time to assemble and they taste as delicious as they look. And since no family cookbook would be complete without a selection of desserts and preserves, I have chosen recipes to appeal to all tastes. Again, they are blissfully easy to prepare and . . . well, why not turn the pages and see for yourself.

Finally, may I offer a suggestion? Next week, take a few minutes to sit down and plan your meals for the whole week. Make a list of ingredients you will need, then shop for everything in one session. This saves time, makes it easier to keep within the housekeeping budget, and the weekly catering runs smoothly.

Cooking for the family can be fun and rewarding. I know that this book will give you lots of new recipe ideas and I hope that you will gain satisfaction and enjoyment from it for years to come.

GOULASH SOUP WITH DUMPLINGS *(page 14)*, VEGETABLE SOUP *(page 19)*, LAMB AND CUCUMBER SOUP *(page 18) (Photograph: New Zealand Lamb Information Bureau)*

SOUPS

Summer Pea Soup

METRIC/IMPERIAL	AMERICAN
40 g/1½ oz butter	3 tablespoons butter
1 onion, chopped	1 onion, chopped
350 g/12 oz fresh or frozen peas	2¼ cups fresh or frozen peas
450 ml/¾ pint chicken stock	2 cups chicken bouillon
2 tablespoons chopped fresh mint	2 tablespoons chopped fresh mint
25 g/1 oz plain flour	¼ cup all-purpose flour
150 ml/¼ pint milk	⅔ cup milk
salt	salt
freshly ground black pepper	freshly ground black pepper

Melt 15 g/½ oz/1 tablespoon of the butter in a saucepan, add the onion and peas, cover and cook over a low heat for 5 minutes, shaking occasionally. Add the stock (bouillon) and half the mint to the peas and onions. Simmer for 30 minutes. Purée in a blender or rub through a sieve.

Heat the remaining butter in a large saucepan, add the flour and cook, stirring, for 2 minutes. Gradually stir in the blended liquid and bring to the boil, stirring continuously.

Stir in the milk and season to taste. Pour into a serving dish and chill.

Garnish with the remaining chopped mint and serve cold.

Serves 4

Cream of Spinach Soup

METRIC/IMPERIAL	AMERICAN
1 × 175 g/6 oz package frozen spinach, thawed	1 × 6 oz package frozen spinach, thawed
50 g/2 oz butter	$\frac{1}{4}$ cup butter
1 onion, chopped	1 onion, chopped
25 g/1 oz plain flour	$\frac{1}{4}$ cup all-purpose flour
pinch of grated nutmeg	pinch grated nutmeg
600 ml/1 pint milk	$2\frac{1}{2}$ cups milk
300 ml/$\frac{1}{2}$ pint chicken stock	$1\frac{1}{4}$ cups chicken bouillon
salt	salt
freshly ground black pepper	freshly ground black pepper
2 tablespoons double cream	2 tablespoons heavy cream

Chop the spinach. Heat the butter in a large saucepan, add the spinach and onion and cook gently for 5 minutes, stirring occasionally.

Blend the flour and nutmeg with the milk and add to the pan with the stock (bouillon), salt and pepper. Bring to the boil, stirring, cover and simmer for 15 minutes.

Taste and adjust the seasoning and pour into a warmed serving dish. Swirl in the cream. Serve hot.

Serves 4

Cool Cucumber Soup

METRIC/IMPERIAL	AMERICAN
15 g/$\frac{1}{2}$ oz butter	1 tablespoon butter
2 onions, chopped	2 onions, chopped
1 medium cucumber	1 medium cucumber
600 ml/1 pint chicken stock	$2\frac{1}{2}$ cups chicken bouillon
450 ml/$\frac{3}{4}$ pint milk	2 cups milk
1 × 142 ml/5 fl oz carton natural yogurt	$\frac{2}{3}$ cup natural yogurt
salt	salt
freshly ground black pepper	freshly ground black pepper

Heat the butter in a large saucepan and gently fry the onion until soft but not browned.

Cut a few thin slices from the cucumber and reserve. Chop the remaining cucumber, add to onions with the stock (bouillon); simmer for 20 minutes.

Purée the soup in a blender or rub through a sieve. Pour into a serving dish, whisk in the milk and yogurt. Season with salt and pepper.

Chill well. Garnish with the reserved cucumber slices and serve cold.

Serves 4 to 6

Country Vegetable Soup

METRIC/IMPERIAL

500 g/1 lb mixed fresh vegetables:
  potatoes, carrots, celery, cauliflower
  etc
50 g/2 oz butter
1 onion, chopped
300 ml/½ pint chicken stock
1 bay leaf
1 sprig fresh rosemary
1 sprig fresh sage
salt
freshly ground black pepper
600 ml/1 pint milk
To Garnish:
1 tablespoon chopped fresh parsley

AMERICAN

1 lb fresh mixed vegetables: potatoes,
  carrots, celery, cauliflower etc
¼ cup butter
1 onion, chopped
1¼ cups chicken bouillon
1 bay leaf
1 sprig fresh rosemary
1 sprig fresh sage
salt
freshly ground black pepper
2½ cups milk
To Garnish:
1 tablespoon chopped fresh parsley

Wash and trim the vegetables and cut into small pieces.

Melt the butter in a large saucepan, add the chopped onion and vegetables and fry for 5 minutes. Add the stock (bouillon), bay leaf, rosemary and sage, and salt and pepper. Bring to the boil, cover and simmer for 35 minutes.

Purée the soup in a blender or rub through a sieve. Return the soup to the pan and add the milk. Bring to the boil and adjust the seasoning. Pour into a warmed serving dish, garnish with the parsley and serve hot.

Serves 4

COUNTRY VEGETABLE SOUP
(Photograph: Cadbury Typhoo Food Advisory Service)

Goulash Soup with Dumplings

METRIC/IMPERIAL

2 tablespoons oil
500 g/1 lb boned shoulder of lamb, cubed
1 onion, sliced
1 clove garlic, crushed
225 g/8 oz tomatoes, skinned and chopped
600 ml/1 pint chicken stock
2 tablespoons paprika
salt
freshly ground black pepper
Dumplings:
100 g/4 oz self-raising flour
pinch of salt
50 g/2 oz shredded suet
1 tablespoon chopped fresh parsley

AMERICAN

2 tablespoons oil
1 lb boned and diced shoulder of lamb
1 onion, sliced
1 clove garlic, crushed
1 cup skinned and chopped tomatoes
$2\frac{1}{2}$ cups chicken bouillon
2 tablespoons paprika
salt
freshly ground black pepper
Dumplings:
1 cup self-rising flour
pinch of salt
$\frac{1}{4}$ cup shredded suet
1 tablespoon chopped fresh parsley

Heat the oil in a large saucepan. Add the lamb and fry until evenly browned. Add the onion and garlic and fry for 5 minutes. Stir in the tomatoes, stock (bouillon), paprika, salt and pepper and bring to the boil. Cover and simmer for 1 hour.

To make the dumplings, sift the flour and salt into a large bowl. Stir in the suet and enough cold water to make a stiff dough. Divide into 12 pieces and shape each into a ball. Add to the simmering soup and cook for a further 15 minutes. Adjust the seasoning, pour into a warmed serving dish, sprinkle with parsley and serve hot.

Serves 4

Chunky Chicken Soup

METRIC/IMPERIAL	AMERICAN
25 g/1 oz butter	2 tablespoons butter
50 g/2 oz streaky bacon, derinded and chopped	3 fatty bacon slices, derinded and chopped
1 onion, chopped	$\frac{1}{2}$ cup chopped onion
225 g/8 oz carrots, chopped	2 cups chopped carrot
2 sticks of celery, chopped	2 sticks celery, chopped
25 g/1 oz pearl barley	$\frac{1}{4}$ cup pearl barley
1.75 litres/3 pints chicken stock	$7\frac{1}{2}$ cups chicken bouillon
1 bay leaf	1 bay leaf
175 g/6 oz cooked chicken, diced	$\frac{3}{4}$ cup diced cooked chicken
salt	salt
freshly ground black pepper	freshly ground black pepper
To Garnish:	**To Garnish:**
1 tablespoon chopped fresh parsley	1 tablespoon chopped fresh parsley

Heat the butter in a large saucepan and fry the bacon until golden. Add the vegetables and cook for 5 minutes. Stir in the pearl barley, stock (bouillon) and bay leaf. Bring to the boil, cover and simmer for 30 minutes.

Add the chicken and salt and pepper to taste and simmer for a further 15 minutes. Pour into a warmed serving dish, sprinkle with parsley and serve hot.

Serves 4

Velvet Soup

METRIC/IMPERIAL	AMERICAN
50 g/2 oz butter	$\frac{1}{4}$ cup butter
75 g/3 oz plain flour	$\frac{3}{4}$ cup all-purpose flour
1.25 litres/2$\frac{1}{4}$ pints beef stock	5$\frac{3}{4}$ cups beef bouillon
175 g/6 oz Gruyère cheese, grated	1$\frac{1}{2}$ cups grated Gruyère cheese
120 ml/4 fl oz milk	$\frac{1}{2}$ cup milk
salt	salt
freshly ground black pepper	freshly ground black pepper
pinch of grated nutmeg	pinch of grated nutmeg

Melt the butter in a large pan, add the flour and cook, stirring continuously, for 2 minutes.

Gradually stir in the stock (bouillon), add salt and pepper and bring to the boil stirring continuously. Simmer gently for 20 minutes, stirring occasionally. Mix 100 g/4 oz/1 cup of the cheese with the milk in the bottom of a warmed soup tureen or large serving bowl. Adjust seasoning, to taste. Pour the simmering soup over the cheese and milk and stir quickly to blend. Sprinkle with the remaining grated cheese and the nutmeg, and serve immediately with hot crusty bread.

Serves 4

Cream of Almond Soup

METRIC/IMPERIAL	AMERICAN
65 g/2$\frac{1}{2}$ oz blanched almonds	$\frac{1}{2}$ cup whole shelled almonds
750 ml/1$\frac{1}{4}$ pints milk	3 cups milk
$\frac{1}{2}$ small onion	$\frac{1}{2}$ small onion
2 sticks of celery	2 celery stalks
25 g/1 oz butter	2 tablespoons butter
15 g/$\frac{1}{2}$ oz plain flour	1 tablespoon all-purpose flour
salt	salt
freshly ground white pepper	freshly ground white pepper
4 tablespoons single cream	4 tablespoons light cream

Chop 40 g/1$\frac{1}{2}$ oz of the almonds finely and place in a saucepan with half the milk and the onion and celery sticks. Simmer for 30 minutes. Remove and discard the vegetables.

Heat half the butter in a large saucepan, add the flour and cook for 2 minutes, stirring. Gradually add the remaining milk and the almond milk, and bring to the boil, stirring continuously. Cover and simmer for 10 minutes. Add salt and pepper to taste.

Cut the remaining almonds into thin slivers and fry in the remaining butter until golden. Pour the soup into a warmed serving dish, stir in the cream, sprinkle the almonds over and serve hot.

Serves 4

VELVET SOUP (Photograph: Cheeses from Switzerland Ltd)

Lamb and Cucumber Soup

METRIC/IMPERIAL	AMERICAN
2 medium cucumbers	*2 medium cucumbers*
1 onion, chopped	*1 onion, chopped*
1.75 litres/3 pints chicken stock	*7½ cups chicken bouillon*
salt	*salt*
freshly ground black pepper	*freshly ground black pepper*
350 g/12 oz shoulder of lamb, minced	*1½ cups ground shoulder of lamb*
50 g/2 oz butter	*¼ cup butter*
2 tablespoons plain flour	*2 tablespoons all-purpose flour*

Peel the cucumbers and cut into 1 cm/¼ in slices. Place in a saucepan with the onion, stock (bouillon) and salt and pepper. Bring to the boil and simmer for 20 minutes. Purée in a blender or rub through a sieve and reserve.

Season the lamb and shape into 16 meatballs. Heat the butter in a large saucepan, add the flour and cook for 2 minutes, stirring. Add the cucumber mixture and bring to the boil, stirring continuously. Add the meatballs and simmer for 15 minutes. Adjust the seasoning, pour into a warmed serving dish. Serve hot.
Serves 4

Hearty Vegetable Soup

METRIC/IMPERIAL	AMERICAN
100 g/4 oz streaky bacon	*6 fatty bacon slices*
25 g/1 oz butter	*2 tablespoons butter*
2 medium leeks, thinly sliced	*2 medium leeks, thinly sliced*
2 carrots, chopped	*2 carrots, chopped*
600 ml/1 pint water	*2½ cups water*
1 × 400 g/14 oz can tomatoes	*1 × 14 oz can tomatoes*
1 × 447 g/15¾ oz can baked beans	*1 × 15¾ oz can baked beans*
1 teaspoon dried mixed herbs	*1 teaspoon dried mixed herbs*
salt	*salt*
freshly ground black pepper	*freshly ground black pepper*

Cut off the rind from the bacon and reserve. Chop the bacon.

Heat the butter in a large pan. Add bacon and fry gently for 5 minutes. Add the leeks and carrots and continue frying for a further 5 minutes. Add water, tomatoes, baked beans, herbs, salt and pepper. Bring to the boil, cover pan and simmer gently for 30 minutes.

Meanwhile, fry bacon rinds until very crisp, remove from the pan and crumble into pieces. Pour the soup into a warmed serving dish. Garnish with the crisply fried bacon rinds and serve hot.
Serves 4

Vegetable Soup

METRIC/IMPERIAL
2 tablespoons oil
1 onion, chopped
2 sticks of celery, thickly sliced
1 carrot, cut into sticks
1.6 litres/2¾ pints water
1 bay leaf
1 leek, thickly sliced
1 small cauliflower, cut into florets
6 Brussels sprouts, halved
2 medium potatoes, diced
1 clove garlic, crushed
2 tomatoes, skinned and chopped
salt
freshly ground black pepper
4 tablespoons grated Parmesan cheese

AMERICAN
2 tablespoons oil
½ cup chopped onion
2 stalks celery, thickly sliced
1 carrot, cut into sticks
7 cups water
1 bay leaf
1 leek, thickly sliced
1 small cauliflower, cut into florets
6 Brussels sprouts, halved
2 medium potatoes, diced
1 clove garlic, crushed
2 tomatoes, skinned and chopped
salt
freshly ground black pepper
¼ cup grated Parmesan cheese

Heat the oil in a large saucepan and fry the onion, celery and carrot until golden. Add the water and bay leaf and bring to the boil. Add the leek, cauliflower and sprouts and simmer for 15 minutes. Stir in the potatoes, garlic, tomatoes and salt and pepper to taste.

Simmer for a further 10 minutes, pour into a warmed serving dish, sprinkle with Parmesan cheese and serve hot.

Serves 4

SALADS

French Dressing

METRIC/IMPERIAL
120 ml/4 fl oz oil
2 tablespoons wine vinegar
¼ teaspoon dry mustard
1 clove garlic, crushed (optional)
½ teaspoon sugar
salt
freshly ground black pepper

AMERICAN
½ cup oil
2 tablespoons wine vinegar
¼ teaspoon dry mustard
1 clove garlic, crushed (optional)
½ teaspoon sugar
salt
freshly ground black pepper

Put all the ingredients into a screw-topped jar and shake well until thoroughly blended. The dressing will keep for several weeks. Always shake well before using.
Makes about 175 ml/6 fl oz/¾ cup

Blue Cheese and Pear Salad

METRIC/IMPERIAL
1 lettuce, shredded
1 × 750 g/1½ lb can pear halves, drained
100 g/4 oz black grapes, halved
Dressing:
175 g/6 oz blue cheese, crumbled
120 ml/4 fl oz mayonnaise
120 ml/4 fl oz soured cream
25 g/1 oz chopped nuts
salt
freshly ground black pepper
pinch of cayenne pepper

AMERICAN
1 head lettuce, shredded
1½ lb can pear halves, drained
¼ lb purple grapes, halved
Dressing:
1 cup blue cheese, crumbled
½ cup mayonnaise
½ cup sour cream
¼ cup chopped nuts
salt
freshly ground black pepper
pinch of cayenne pepper

Line a salad bowl with the lettuce and arrange the pear halves on it. Mix all the dressing ingredients together. Spoon over the pear halves to cover them completely. Garnish with the grapes.
Serves 4 to 6

BLUE CHEESE AND PEAR SALAD (Photographer: John Lee)

Tomato Salad

METRIC/IMPERIAL
500 g/1 lb tomatoes, thinly sliced
1 tablespoon chopped fresh basil
½ teaspoon finely grated lemon rind
2 tablespoons French dressing

AMERICAN
2 cups tomatoes, thinly sliced
1 tablespoon chopped fresh basil
½ teaspoon finely grated lemon rind
2 tablespoons French dressing

Arrange the tomato slices decoratively in a shallow dish and sprinkle with the basil and the lemon rind, then pour the dressing over. Chill for 15 minutes.
Serves 4

Orange Mint Salad

METRIC/IMPERIAL
4 oranges, thinly sliced
1 tablespoon chopped fresh mint
5 tablespoons olive oil
1½ tablespoons lemon juice
1½ tablespoons brandy

AMERICAN
4 oranges, thinly sliced
1 tablespoon chopped fresh mint
⅓ cup olive oil
1½ tablespoons lemon juice
1½ tablespoons brandy

Arrange the orange slices in overlapping circles, then sprinkle with mint. Mix all the remaining ingredients together and pour over the oranges.
Serves 4

Cottage Cheese and Nut Salad

METRIC/IMPERIAL
350 g/12 oz cottage cheese
25 g/1 oz chopped nuts
1 dessert apple, cored and diced
2 tablespoons chopped pineapple
salt
freshly ground black pepper
6 lettuce leaves

AMERICAN
1½ cups cottage cheese
¼ cup chopped nuts
1 dessert apple, cored and diced
2 tablespoons chopped pineapple
salt
freshly ground black pepper
6 lettuce leaves

Mix the cheese, nuts and fruit together. Season with salt and pepper. Line a salad bowl with the lettuce leaves and spoon the cheese mixture into the centre.
Serves 4

Spring Salad

METRIC/IMPERIAL
175 g/6 oz cooked green beans, sliced
2 cooked potatoes, thinly sliced
2 spring onions, finely chopped
2 tablespoons olive oil
1 tablespoon vinegar
salt
freshly ground black pepper
150 ml/5 fl oz natural yogurt
2 teaspoons chopped fresh parsley
1 teaspoon chopped fresh mint

AMERICAN
1 cup cooked, sliced green beans
2 cooked potatoes, thinly sliced
2 scallions, finely chopped
2 tablespoons olive oil
1 tablespoon vinegar
salt
freshly ground black pepper
$\frac{2}{3}$ cup unflavored yogurt
2 teaspoons chopped fresh parsley
1 teaspoon chopped fresh mint

Put the green beans, potatoes and spring onions (scallions) into a salad bowl. Add the oil, vinegar and salt and pepper to taste. Toss well to coat. Stir in the yogurt, parsley and mint and toss well.
Serves 4

Pea Salad

METRIC/IMPERIAL
500 g/1 lb cooked peas
100 g/4 oz mushrooms, thinly sliced
2 celery sticks, thinly sliced
2 tablespoons sultanas
2 tablespoons olive oil
2 tablespoons wine vinegar
salt
freshly ground black pepper
$\frac{1}{2}$ teaspoon dry mustard
1 teaspoon sugar
1 clove garlic, crushed

AMERICAN
3 cups cooked peas
1 cup thinly sliced mushrooms
2 celery stalks, thinly sliced
2 tablespoons seedless white raisins
2 tablespoons olive oil
2 tablespoons wine vinegar
salt
freshly ground black pepper
$\frac{1}{2}$ teaspoon dry mustard
1 teaspoon sugar
1 clove garlic, crushed

Mix the peas, mushrooms, celery and sultanas (raisins) together in a salad bowl. Mix the remaining ingredients together, then pour over the vegetables and toss well to coat. Chill for 1 hour.
Serves 6

Red Cabbage Salad

METRIC/IMPERIAL	AMERICAN
250 ml/8 fl oz vinegar	1 cup vinegar
50 g/2 oz sugar	$\frac{1}{2}$ cup sugar
1 clove garlic, crushed	1 clove garlic, crushed
2 bay leaves	2 bay leaves
2 teaspoons peppercorns	2 teaspoons peppercorns
2 teaspoons salt	2 teaspoons salt
1 red cabbage, shredded	1 head red cabbage, shredded
2 large dessert apples, cored and chopped	2 large dessert apples, cored and chopped
2 spring onions, chopped	2 scallions, chopped

Put the vinegar, sugar, garlic, bay leaves, peppercorns and salt into a saucepan. Bring to the boil, stirring continuously. Boil for 2 minutes. Strain.

Put all the remaining ingredients into a salad bowl. Pour the flavoured vinegar over and toss well to coat. Chill for 1 hour. Toss before serving.

Serves 8 to 10

Cucumber and Yogurt Salad

METRIC/IMPERIAL	AMERICAN
1 cucumber, thinly sliced	1 cucumber, thinly sliced
300 ml/$\frac{1}{2}$ pint natural yogurt	1$\frac{1}{4}$ cups unflavored yogurt
salt	salt
freshly ground black pepper	freshly ground black pepper
1 teaspoon paprika	1 teaspoon paprika
2 teaspoons lemon juice	2 teaspoons lemon juice

Put the cucumber in a salad bowl. Mix all the remaining ingredients together, then stir into the cucumber. Chill for 1 hour.

Serves 4 to 6

RED CABBAGE SALAD *(Photographer: Melvin Grey)*

VEGETABLES

Marrow with Tomatoes

METRIC/IMPERIAL
4 tablespoons oil
1 large onion, chopped
4 tomatoes, skinned and chopped
120 ml/4 fl oz tomato juice
salt
freshly ground black pepper
½ teaspoon dried mixed herbs
1 kg/2 lb marrow, peeled, seeded and cubed
50 g/2 oz Parmesan cheese, grated

AMERICAN
4 tablespoons oil
1 large onion, chopped
4 tomatoes, skinned and chopped
½ cup tomato juice
salt
freshly ground black pepper
½ teaspoon dried mixed herbs
2 lb squash, peeled, seeded and cubed
½ cup grated Parmesan cheese

Heat the oil in a saucepan. Add the onion and fry for 5 minutes. Add the tomatoes and fry for 1 minute. Stir in the tomato juice, salt and pepper to taste and the herbs, and cook for 3 minutes. Add the marrow (squash) cubes.

Cover and simmer for 30 minutes, or until the marrow (squash) is tender. Sprinkle with the cheese.
Serves 6 to 8

Cheese and Potato Bake

METRIC/IMPERIAL
750 g/1 lb potatoes, cooked and
  mashed
6 tablespoons milk
25 g/1 oz butter
175 g/6 oz grated cheese
1 egg
salt
freshly ground black pepper

AMERICAN
2 cups cooked and mashed potato
6 tablespoons milk
2 tablespoons butter
1½ cups grated cheese
1 egg
salt
freshly ground black pepper

Mix the ingredients together, except 50 g/2 oz/¼ cup of the cheese for
garnish, season to taste with salt and pepper and spoon into a well-
greased ovenproof dish. Top with the reserved grated cheese and put
into a preheated fairly hot oven (190°C/375°F, Gas Mark 5). Bake for
about 25 minutes, or until golden brown on top.
Serves 4

Braised Celery

METRIC/IMPERIAL
2 small heads celery, trimmed,
  blanched for 10 minutes in boiling
  water and drained
300 ml/½ pint chicken stock
15 g/½ oz butter
1 small onion, chopped
1 tablespoon plain flour
salt
freshly ground black pepper
paprika

AMERICAN
2 small heads celery, trimmed,
  blanched for 10 minutes in boiling
  water and drained
1¼ cups chicken bouillon
1 tablespoon butter
1 small onion, chopped
1 tablespoon all-purpose flour
salt
freshly ground black pepper
paprika

Tie up the blanched celery heads and put in a saucepan with the stock
(bouillon). Cover and bring to the boil. Simmer for 20 minutes until
tender. Drain, remove the string and keep the celery hot. Reserve
300 ml/½ pint/1¼ cups of the cooking liquid, making up this amount with
water if necessary.
   Melt the butter in a saucepan. Add the onion and fry for 5 minutes.
Stir in the flour to form a smooth paste, then gradually stir in the
reserved stock. Bring to the boil, stirring continuously. Cook for 2 to 3
minutes, or until the sauce thickens. Season to taste with the salt and
pepper, pour sauce over the celery and sprinkle with paprika.
Serves 4

Cauliflower Basket

METRIC/IMPERIAL

1 hot cooked cauliflower, drained and
  150 ml/¼ pint cooking liquid
  reserved

Sauce:

25 g/1 oz butter
25 g/1 oz flour
150 ml/¼ pint milk
salt
freshly ground black pepper
100 g/4 oz Cheddar cheese grated
2 hard boiled eggs, chopped
1 tablespoon chopped gherkins
1 tablespoon chopped fresh parsley
1 tablespoon chopped chives

AMERICAN

1 hot cooked cauliflower, drained and
  ⅔ cup cooking liquid reserved

Sauce:

2 tablespoons butter
¼ cup all-purpose flour
⅔ cup milk
salt
freshly ground black pepper
1 cup grated Cheddar type cheese
2 hard boiled eggs, chopped
1 tablespoon chopped small sweet dill
  pickle
1 tablespoon chopped fresh parsley
1 tablespoon chopped chives

To make the sauce, melt the butter in a saucepan. Stir in the flour to form a smooth paste. Gradually add the milk and reserved cooking liquid and bring to the boil, stirring continuously. Season with salt and pepper and stir in nearly all the cheese.

Mix together the eggs, gherkins (dill pickle), parsley and chives. Scoop out the centre of the cauliflower and chop coarsely. Add this to the egg mixture and stir it all into the sauce.

Stand the cauliflower in a heated flameproof serving dish and pile the cheese sauce mixture into the centre. Top with the remainder of the cheese and grill (broil) for 2 to 3 minutes or until the top is lightly browned.

Serves 4

CAULIFLOWER BASKET *(Photographer: John Lee)*

Potatoes Anna

METRIC/IMPERIAL	AMERICAN
1 kg/2 lb potatoes, very thinly sliced	*2 cups very thinly sliced potato*
125 g/4 oz butter, softened	*½ cup softened butter*
salt	*salt*
freshly ground black pepper	*freshly ground black pepper*
To Garnish:	**To Garnish:**
chopped parsley	*chopped parsley*

Chill the potato slices in iced water for 30 minutes. Drain and dry well. Place a layer of potato over the base of a generously buttered baking dish. Spread over some of the softened butter. Season lightly with salt and pepper.

Repeat layers of potato, butter and seasoning, ending with a layer of butter. Put the dish into a preheated hot oven (220°C/425°F, Gas Mark 7) and bake for 45 to 55 minutes, or until the potatoes are soft. Turn out on to a warmed serving dish and garnish with parsley.
Serves 4

Leeks in Cheese Sauce

METRIC/IMPERIAL	AMERICAN
25 g/1 oz butter	*2 tablespoons butter*
25 g/1 oz plain flour	*¼ cup all-purpose flour*
300 ml/½ pint milk	*1¼ cups milk*
100 g/4 oz cheese, grated	*1 cup grated cheese*
salt	*salt*
freshly ground black pepper	*freshly ground black pepper*
4 hot cooked leeks, drained	*4 hot cooked leeks, drained*

Melt the butter in a saucepan and stir in the flour to form a smooth paste. Gradually add the milk and bring to the boil, stirring continuously. Cook for 2 to 3 minutes, or until the sauce thickens. Add most of the cheese and salt and pepper to taste. Stir well until the cheese has melted.

Arrange the leeks in a shallow flameproof dish and pour over the sauce. Sprinkle with the remaining cheese. Grill (broil) for 5 minutes, or until the top is golden brown.
Serves 4

Stuffed Courgettes

METRIC/IMPERIAL	AMERICAN
1 large slice of bread, crusts removed	1 large slice of bread, crusts removed
milk	milk
500 g/1 lb courgettes	1 lb zucchini
4 mushrooms, chopped	4 mushrooms, chopped
2 anchovy fillets, chopped	2 anchovy fillets, chopped
2 bacon rashers, chopped	2 bacon slices, chopped
3 tablespoons grated Parmesan cheese	3 tablespoons grated Parmesan cheese
1 teaspoon chopped fresh basil	1 teaspoon chopped fresh basil
salt	salt
freshly ground black pepper	freshly ground black pepper
1 egg yolk	1 egg yolk
2 teaspoons fresh breadcrumbs	2 teaspoons fresh bread crumbs
oil	oil

Soak the bread for 10 minutes in a little milk, then squeeze dry.

Blanch the courgettes (zucchini) in boiling salted water for 3 minutes and drain. Cut in half lengthways and scoop out the flesh.

Mix together the mushrooms, anchovy fillets, bacon, 2 tablespoons of the cheese, basil, bread and courgette (zucchini) flesh. Season with salt and pepper to taste and bind together with the egg yolk. Fill the courgette (zucchini) halves with this mixture and arrange them in a lightly-oiled ovenproof dish.

Mix the remaining cheese with the breadcrumbs and sprinkle over the top. Sprinkle with a little oil and put into a preheated moderate oven (180°C/350°F, Gas Mark 4). Bake for 40 minutes, or until the courgettes (zucchini) are tender.
Serves 4

Runner Beans with Carrots

METRIC/IMPERIAL	AMERICAN
225 g/8 oz carrots, thinly sliced	2 cups thinly sliced carrots
salt	salt
freshly ground black pepper	freshly ground black pepper
500 g/1 lb runner beans, thinly sliced	2 cups thinly sliced French beans
2 tablespoons oil	2 tablespoons oil

Put the carrots in a saucepan and cover with 2.5 cm/1 in of water. Season with salt and pepper, cover and cook for 10 minutes. Add the beans and oil and continue cooking for a further 20 minutes or until the vegetables are very tender and most of the water has evaporated. Drain off any remaining water.
Serves 4

Asparagus with Hollandaise Sauce

METRIC/IMPERIAL
1 bunch asparagus spears
salt
Hollandaise Sauce:
3 tablespoons wine vinegar
6 peppercorns
½ bay leaf
2 egg yolks
100 g/4 oz butter, softened
salt
freshly ground black pepper
lemon juice

AMERICAN
1 bunch asparagus spears
salt
Hollandaise Sauce:
3 tablespoons wine vinegar
6 peppercorns
½ bay leaf
2 egg yolks
½ cup softened butter
salt
freshly ground black pepper
lemon juice

Cut off the tough ends of the asparagus spears so that they are all about the same length. Scrape off the skin at the cut end for about 2.5 cm/1 in. Wash the spears and tie them into a bundle.

Bring a saucepan of salted water to the boil and stand the asparagus in it so that the tips are above the water. Cover with foil and simmer for 12 to 15 minutes, or until the asparagus is tender. Carefully lift out, drain and untie the spears.

Serve hot with the Hollandaise sauce.

To make the Hollandaise sauce, simmer the vinegar, peppercorns and bay leaf together until the liquid is reduced by half. Cool and strain.

Beat the egg yolks with a knob of the butter and a pinch of salt and pepper in the top of a double boiler. Gradually stir in the strained vinegar. Stir over simmering water until the sauce has just begun to thicken. Add the remaining butter in small pieces, stirring continuously.

When all the butter has been added, add lemon juice to taste. Pour over the asparagus.

Serves 3

ASPARAGUS WITH HOLLANDAISE SAUCE *(Photographer: John Lee)*

MEAT

Stuffed Breast of Lamb

METRIC/IMPERIAL
100 g/4 oz streaky bacon, derinded
  and chopped
75 g/3 oz fresh breadcrumbs
50 g/2 oz mushrooms, chopped
75 g/3 oz pickled walnuts, drained
1 egg
1 kg/2 lb breast of lamb, boned
salt
freshly ground black pepper
To Garnish:
tomato waterlilies and fresh parsley
  sprigs

AMERICAN
6 fatty bacon slices, derinded
  and chopped
1½ cups fresh bread crumbs
½ cup chopped mushrooms
¾ cup drained and sliced pickled
  walnuts
1 egg
2 lb breast of lamb, boned
salt
freshly ground black pepper
To Garnish:
tomato waterlilies and fresh parsley
  sprigs

Mix together the bacon, breadcrumbs, mushrooms and pickled walnuts.
Add the egg and mix together until they are well combined.

Lay breast of lamb, skin side down, on a board and sprinkle with salt
and pepper. Spread the stuffing evenly over the lamb. Roll up and tie
with fine string at regular intervals.

Put into a roasting tin and cook in a preheated moderate oven
(180°C/350°F, Gas Mark 4) for 1¼ to 1½ hours until tender.

Transfer to a warmed serving dish, garnish with tomatoes and parsley
and serve hot or cold cut into slices.
Serves 4

34

Lamb Parcels

METRIC/IMPERIAL
4 lamb chops, trimmed
salt
freshly ground black pepper
½ teaspoon made mustard
1 teaspoon dried thyme
25 g/1 oz butter or margarine
1 onion, sliced
1 green pepper, halved and sliced
1 teaspoon vinegar
2 teaspoons soy sauce
2 canned pineapple rings, chopped
1 teaspoon plain flour
120 ml/4 fl oz chicken stock
To Garnish:
sprigs of fresh mint

AMERICAN
4 lamb chops, trimmed
salt
freshly ground black pepper
½ teaspoon mustard
1 teaspoon dried thyme
2 tablespoons butter or margarine
1 onion, sliced
1 green pepper, halved and sliced
1 teaspoon vinegar
2 teaspoons soy sauce
2 canned pineapple rings, chopped
1 teaspoon all-purpose flour
½ cup chicken bouillon
To Garnish:
sprigs of fresh mint

Place each chop on a piece of foil. Sprinkle with salt and pepper and spread the mustard over; sprinkle with thyme.

Heat the butter or margarine in a saucepan and fry the onion and pepper. Add the vinegar, soy sauce and pineapple. Blend the flour with the stock (bouillon) and stir into the pan. Bring to the boil, stirring, and cook for 2 to 3 minutes.

Divide the mixture between the parcels, spreading it over the chops. Fold the foil around the chops, sealing well. Bake in a moderate oven (180°C/350°F, Gas Mark 4) for 1 hour.

Remove the chops from the foil parcels and arrange on a warmed serving plate. Adjust seasoning. Garnish with sprigs of fresh mint and serve hot.

Serves 4

Lamb Curry

METRIC/IMPERIAL
50 g/2 oz flour
2 teaspoons salt
750 g/1½ lb boned shoulder of lamb,
  cubed
50 g/2 oz dripping
2 onions, chopped
1 clove garlic, crushed
2 apples, peeled and sliced
1 tomato, skinned and chopped
4 teaspoons curry powder
450 ml/¾ pint chicken stock
grated rind and juice of ½ a lemon
1 teaspoon sugar
1 tablespoon flaked almonds
2 tablespoons raisins
To Garnish:
lemon slices

AMERICAN
½ cup all-purpose flour
2 teaspoons salt
1½ lb boned shoulder of lamb, cubed
¼ cup drippings
2 onions, chopped
1 clove garlic, crushed
2 apples, peeled and sliced
1 tomato, skinned and chopped
4 teaspoons curry powder
2 cups chicken bouillon
grated rind and juice of ½ a lemon
1 teaspoon sugar
1 tablespoon slivered almonds
2 tablespoons raisins
To Garnish:
lemon slices

Mix the flour and salt together and toss the lamb in it until evenly coated. Heat the dripping in a large saucepan and fry the lamb until browned. Add the onions, garlic, apple and tomato and fry for 5 minutes. Add any remaining flour and the curry powder and gradually stir in the stock (bouillon). Bring to the boil, stirring continuously.

Add the lemon rind and juice, sugar, almonds and raisins. Cover and simmer for 1½ hours.

Adjust the seasoning and serve with boiled rice. Garnish with lemon slices.
Serves 4

LAMB CURRY (*Photograph: New Zealand Lamb Information Bureau*)

Beef Olives with Walnuts

METRIC/IMPERIAL

1 small head of celery
4 × 100 g/4 oz thin slices braising
  steak
100 g/4 oz beansprouts
25 g/1 oz walnuts, chopped
½ teaspoon ground ginger
2 tablespoons fresh breadcrumbs
50 g/2 oz butter or margarine, melted
salt
freshly ground black pepper
2 tablespoons plain flour
300 ml/½ pint beef stock
To Garnish:
sprigs of fresh parsley

AMERICAN

1 small head of celery
4 × 4 oz thin slices braising steak
2 cups beansprouts
¼ cup chopped walnuts
½ teaspoon ground ginger
2 tablespoons fresh bread crumbs
¼ cup melted butter or margarine
salt
freshly ground black pepper
2 tablespoons all-purpose flour
1¼ cups beef bouillon
To Garnish:
sprigs of fresh parsley

Wash and trim celery and remove outer sticks (stalks). Chop 4 stalks finely, cut the remaining sticks (stalks) into 7.5 cm/3 in lengths and reserve.

Beat out the slices of meat thinly between sheets of damp greaseproof (wax) paper.

Mix together the beansprouts, walnuts, chopped celery, ginger and breadcrumbs with half the melted fat. Spread the filling over the meat slices, season well with salt and pepper, roll up into neat parcels and secure with fine string. Coat the rolls in seasoned flour.

Heat the remaining fat in a frying pan (skillet) and fry the beef rolls, turning frequently until brown all over. Remove from the pan.

Stir the remaining seasoned flour into the fat left in the pan and cook, stirring for 2 minutes. Gradually add the stock (bouillon). Bring to the boil, stirring continuously. Return the rolls to the pan, cover and simmer for about 30 minutes, or until the beef is tender.

Meanwhile, cook the reserved sticks (stalks) of celery in lightly salted water 5 to 10 minutes until tender.

Remove the string from the beef olives and arrange on a warmed serving dish. Garnish with the cooked celery and parsley and serve hot.
Serves 4

Chilli (Chili) con Carne

METRIC/IMPERIAL
350 g/12 oz red kidney beans, soaked
  overnight
25 g/1 oz butter or margarine
1 large onion, chopped
500 g/1 lb minced beef
1 × 400 g/14 oz can tomatoes
2 tablespoons tomato purée
1 to 2 teaspoons chilli powder
150 ml/¼ pint beef stock
salt

AMERICAN
1 cup red kidney beans, soaked
  overnight
2 tablespoons butter or margarine
1 large onion, chopped
2 firmly packed cups ground beef
1 × 14 oz can tomatoes
2 tablespoons tomato paste
1 to 2 teaspoons chili powder
⅔ cup beef bouillon
salt

Place the beans in a pan of boiling water and cook for 1 hour until just tender. Drain and reserve.

Heat the fat in a large saucepan and fry the onion and beef until brown. Add the canned tomatoes and juice, tomato paste, chilli (chili) powder, beef stock (bouillon) and salt and bring to the boil. Cover and simmer for 30 minutes. Adjust the seasoning and serve hot.
Serves 4

Liver Provençale

METRIC/IMPERIAL
500 g/1 lb lambs' liver, sliced
15 g/½ oz plain flour, seasoned with
  salt and pepper
25 g/1 oz butter or margarine
2 rashers bacon, derinded and chopped
1 onion, sliced
225 g/8 oz can tomatoes
1 bay leaf
2 teaspoons Worcestershire sauce
5 tablespoons stock
salt
freshly ground black pepper

AMERICAN
1 lb lambs' liver, sliced
2 tablespoons all-purpose flour,
  seasoned with salt and pepper
2 tablespoons butter or margarine
2 slices bacon, derinded and chopped
1 onion, sliced
1 × ½ lb can tomatoes
1 bay leaf
2 teaspoons Worcestershire sauce
⅓ cup bouillon
salt
freshly ground black pepper

Coat the liver with seasoned flour. Heat the butter or margarine in a flameproof casserole and fry the liver, bacon and onion for 2 to 3 minutes. Add the canned tomatoes and their juice, bay leaf, Worcestershire sauce, stock (bouillon) and salt and pepper. Bring to the boil, stirring continuously. Cover and cook in a moderate oven (160°C/325°F, Gas Mark 3) for ¾ hour. Serve with boiled rice and a green salad.
Serves 4

Liver Casserole

METRIC/IMPERIAL	AMERICAN
1 tablespoon oil	1 tablespoon oil
25 g/1 oz seasoned flour	$\frac{1}{4}$ cup seasoned flour
350 g/12 oz lambs' liver, thinly sliced	$\frac{3}{4}$ lb lambs' liver, thinly sliced
3 rashers bacon, derinded	3 slices bacon, derinded
175 g/6 oz smoked sausage, sliced	6 oz smoked sausage, sliced
600 ml/1 pint French onion soup	$2\frac{1}{2}$ cups French onion soup
1 × 15 ml/1 tablespoon tomato purée	1 tablespoon tomato paste

Heat oil in a flameproof casserole. Flour the liver and fry gently for about 5 minutes.

Cut each bacon rasher into 4, add to pan and cook for a further 5 minutes. Add the sliced sausage.

Add the onion soup and purée (paste) to the casserole. Bring to the boil, stirring. Cover and simmer for 5 minutes. Serve hot with creamed potatoes and green vegetables.

Serves 4

Pepperpot Casserole

METRIC/IMPERIAL	AMERICAN
2 large onions	2 large onions
4 small courgettes	4 small zucchini
2 green peppers	2 green peppers
1 celery heart	1 celery heart
3 tablespoons oil	3 tablespoons oil
750 g/1$\frac{1}{2}$ lb stewing steak	1$\frac{1}{2}$ lb stewing steak
25 g/1 oz plain flour	$\frac{1}{4}$ cup all-purpose flour
2 teaspoons salt	2 teaspoons salt
300 ml/$\frac{1}{2}$ pint beef stock	1$\frac{1}{4}$ cups beef bouillon
grated rind and juice of 1 orange	grated rind and juice of 1 orange

Cut each onion into 8 wedges. Thickly slice the courgettes (zucchini). Deseed the peppers and cut each into 8 pieces, then thickly slice the celery heart. Heat the oil in a flameproof casserole and fry the vegetables until golden brown. Remove from the pan and reserve.

Cut the meat into chunky pieces, toss in the flour and salt; fry in the casserole until brown all over, turning frequently.

Return the vegetables to the pan and add the stock (bouillon). Stir in the orange rind and juice, cover and cook in a preheated moderate oven (160°C/325°F, Gas Mark 3) for about 1$\frac{1}{2}$ hours, until the meat is tender.

Adjust seasoning and serve hot with jacket potatoes.

Serves 4

PEPPERPOT CASSEROLE (Photograph: Fyffes Group)

Veal Paprika

METRIC/IMPERIAL

500 g/1 lb pie veal, cubed
1 tablespoon plain flour
1 tablespoon paprika
salt
freshly ground black pepper
50 g/2 oz butter or margarine
1 onion, chopped
175 ml/6 fl oz chicken stock
2 sticks celery, chopped
100 g/4 oz tomatoes, skinned and
  chopped
1 tablespoon tomato purée
To Garnish:
1 tablespoon chopped fresh parsley
  and a pinch of paprika

AMERICAN

1 lb pie veal, cubed
1 tablespoon all-purpose flour
1 tablespoon paprika
salt
freshly ground black pepper
$\frac{1}{4}$ cup butter or margarine
1 onion, chopped
$\frac{3}{4}$ cup chicken bouillon
2 stalks celery, chopped
$\frac{1}{2}$ cup skinned and chopped tomatoes
1 tablespoon tomato paste
To Garnish:
1 tablespoon chopped fresh parsley
  and a pinch of paprika

Toss the veal in the flour, paprika, salt and pepper. Heat the butter or margarine in a large frying pan (skillet). Add the veal and fry with the onion for 5 minutes. Stir in any remaining flour and cook for 2 minutes, stirring continuously. Gradually stir in the stock (bouillon) and bring to the boil, stirring continuously. Add the celery, tomatoes and tomato purée (paste). Add salt and pepper and transfer to a casserole.

Bake in a preheated moderate oven (180°C/350°F, Gas Mark 4) for 1$\frac{1}{2}$ hours until meat is tender. Adjust seasoning, garnish with chopped parsley and paprika and serve hot.
Serves 4

Pork Wellington

METRIC/IMPERIAL	AMERICAN
25 g/1 oz butter	2 tablespoons butter
2 pork fillets	2 pork tenderloins
1 onion, chopped	1 onion, chopped
3 rashers streaky bacon, chopped	3 fatty bacon slices, chopped
225 g/8 oz mushrooms, chopped	2 cups chopped mushrooms
1 teaspoon dried mixed herbs	1 teaspoon dried mixed herbs
salt	salt
freshly ground black pepper	freshly ground black pepper
1 tablespoon chopped fresh parsley	1 tablespoon chopped fresh parsley
1 × 375 g/13 oz package frozen puff pastry, thawed	13 oz package frozen puff pastry, thawed
1 egg, beaten	1 egg, beaten
To Garnish:	**To Garnish:**
watercress and fried mushrooms	watercress and fried mushrooms

Heat the butter in a frying pan and brown the pork. Set aside to cool. Add the onion, bacon and mushrooms to the pan, add the herbs, salt and pepper and cook until golden. Stir in the parsley and leave to cool.

Roll out the pastry to a rectangle large enough to wrap around the pork. Place the fillets (tenderloins) along the centre, leaving a wide border all round. Cover with the mushroom mixture, brush the pastry edges with beaten egg and fold the pastry over the filling to enclose it. Brush with beaten egg to seal and glaze the pastry.

Bake in a preheated hot oven (230°C/450°F, Gas Mark 8) for 10 minutes, reduce the heat to moderately hot (200°C/400°F, Gas Mark 6) for 30 minutes until well risen and golden.

Transfer to a warmed serving plate. Garnish with watercress and fried mushrooms and serve hot.

Serves 6 to 8

Pork Chops with Cabbage

METRIC/IMPERIAL	AMERICAN
750 g/1½ lb cabbage	1½ lb cabbage
salt	salt
25 g/1 oz butter	2 tablespoons butter
1 large onion, chopped	1 large onion, chopped
1 clove of garlic, crushed	1 clove of garlic, crushed
4 pork chops	4 pork chops
freshly ground black pepper	freshly ground black pepper
300 ml/½ pint cider	1½ cups hard cider
4 tablespoons double cream	4 tablespoons heavy cream
50 g/2 oz cheese, grated	½ cup grated cheese

Finely shred the cabbage and cook in boiling salted water for 5 minutes. Drain thoroughly and place in a large bowl. Melt half the butter in a frying pan (skillet), add the onion and garlic and fry until golden. Add the onion and pan juices to the cabbage with salt and pepper. Mix lightly and spread half over the bottom of an ovenproof dish.

Heat the remaining butter in the frying pan (skillet), season the chops with salt and pepper and fry quickly on both sides until golden brown. Remove from the pan and place on the cabbage in the casserole. Cover with the remaining cabbage. Pour the cider into the frying pan (skillet) and boil rapidly until reduced by half.

Remove from the heat, stir in the cream and pour over the cabbage. Cover and bake in a preheated moderate oven (180°C/350°F, Gas Mark 4) for 45 minutes. Remove the lid, sprinkle the cheese on top and cook for a further 15 minutes until golden and serve hot.

Serves 4

PORK CHOPS WITH CABBAGE *(Photograph: Taunton Cider)*

North Country Kidney Casserole

<table>
<tr><td>METRIC/IMPERIAL</td><td>AMERICAN</td></tr>
<tr><td>40 g/1½ oz butter or margarine</td><td>3 tablespoons butter or margarine</td></tr>
<tr><td>1 onion, sliced</td><td>1 onion, sliced</td></tr>
<tr><td>500 g/1 lb pigs' kidneys cored and chopped</td><td>1 lb pork kidneys, cored and chopped</td></tr>
<tr><td>15 g/½ oz plain flour seasoned with salt and pepper</td><td>1 tablespoon all-purpose flour seasoned with salt and pepper</td></tr>
<tr><td>100 g/4 oz button mushrooms, sliced</td><td>1 cup button mushrooms, sliced</td></tr>
<tr><td>1 × 400 g/14 oz can tomatoes</td><td>1 × 14 oz can tomatoes</td></tr>
<tr><td>salt</td><td>salt</td></tr>
<tr><td>freshly ground black pepper</td><td>freshly ground black pepper</td></tr>
<tr><td>75 g/3 oz fresh breadcrumbs</td><td>1½ cups fresh bread crumbs</td></tr>
<tr><td>1 teaspoon dried mixed herbs</td><td>1 teaspoon dried mixed herbs</td></tr>
<tr><td>1 egg, beaten</td><td>1 egg, beaten</td></tr>
<tr><td>**To Garnish:**</td><td>**To Garnish:**</td></tr>
<tr><td>1 tablespoon chopped fresh parsley</td><td>1 tablespoon chopped fresh parsley</td></tr>
</table>

Melt 25 g/1 oz/2 tablespoons of the butter in a flameproof casserole and fry the onion. Coat the chopped kidneys with the seasoned flour. Add to the onions with the mushrooms and fry for 3 minutes until brown.

Add the remaining flour and cook for 2 minutes. Gradually add the canned tomatoes and their juice. Bring to the boil, stirring continuously. Add salt and pepper to taste.

Melt the remaining butter, add the breadcrumbs, herbs and beaten egg and stir to a soft dough mixture. Shape the mixture into 8 balls and arrange round the edge of the casserole.

Cover and bake in a moderate oven (180°C/350°F, Gas Mark 4) for 40 minutes. Remove lid and cook for a further 10 minutes to brown the dumplings. Sprinkle with chopped parsley and serve hot.

Serves 4

Midweek Savoury

METRIC/IMPERIAL

1 kg/2 lb gammon knuckle
350 g/12 oz split peas, soaked
  overnight
25 g/1 oz butter
1 large onion, chopped
2 tablespoons plain flour
450 ml/¾ pint stock
salt
freshly ground black pepper
2 teaspoons yeast extract
To Garnish:
1 tablespoon chopped fresh parsley

AMERICAN

2 lb gammon knuckle
1½ cups split peas, soaked overnight
2 tablespoons butter
1 large onion, chopped
2 tablespoons all-purpose flour
2 cups bouillon
salt
freshly ground black pepper
2 teaspoons yeast extract
To Garnish:
1 tablespoon chopped fresh parsley

Place the gammon knuckle in a large pan, cover with cold water and bring to the boil. Pour off the water and cover with fresh cold water. Add the well drained split peas.

Bring slowly to the boil and cook for 1¼ hours. Remove the gammon, remove and discard the rind and dice the meat. Drain the peas, reserving the stock (bouillon).

Heat the butter in a large pan and fry the onion until golden. Add the flour and cook, stirring, for 2 minutes. Gradually add the stock (bouillon) and salt and pepper and bring to the boil, stirring continuously. Add the yeast extract and cook for 1 minute.

Add the split peas and bacon to the sauce and cook gently for 10 minutes. Transfer to a warmed serving dish, garnish with parsley and serve with French bread.

Serves 6

Pork Chop and Apple Bake

METRIC/IMPERIAL
750 g/1½ lb potatoes, peeled and diced
4 pork chops
salt
freshly ground black pepper
2 onions, thinly sliced
225 g/8 oz cooking apples, peeled,
 cored and sliced
½ teaspoon ground coriander
2 tablespoons sugar
4 tablespoons cider or apple juice
75 g/3 oz cheese, grated
25 g/1 oz butter
To Garnish:
sprigs of fresh parsley

AMERICAN
4 cups peeled and diced potatoes
4 pork chops
salt
freshly ground black pepper
2 onions, thinly sliced
2 cups peeled, cored and sliced cooking
 apples
½ teaspoon ground coriander
2 tablespoons sugar
4 tablespoons hard cider or apple
 juice
¾ cup grated cheese
2 tablespoons butter
To Garnish:
sprigs of fresh parsley

Cook the diced potatoes in salted water for 10 minutes. Drain
thoroughly.

Trim the pork chops, removing surplus fat. Place in a greased
ovenproof dish. Sprinkle with salt and freshly ground pepper. Cover
with the onions, then the sliced apple. Sprinkle with ground coriander
and sugar. Add the cider or apple juice. Top the chops with the diced
potatoes; sprinkle with grated cheese and dot with butter.

Cover with foil and bake in a preheated moderately hot oven
(190°C/375°F, Gas Mark 5) for 30 minutes.

Remove the foil and bake for a further 25 minutes until the pork is
tender and the topping crisp and golden. Adjust seasoning, garnish with
parsley sprigs and serve hot.
Serves 4

PORK CHOP AND APPLE BAKE
(Photograph: Apple and Pear Development Council)

POULTRY

Chicken Risotto

METRIC/IMPERIAL	AMERICAN
25 g/1 oz butter	2 tablespoons butter
1 onion, chopped	1 onion, chopped
50 g/2 oz streaky bacon, chopped	3 fatty bacon slices, chopped
175 g/6 oz long-grain rice	$\frac{7}{8}$ cup long-grain rice
600 ml/1 pint chicken stock	$2\frac{1}{2}$ cups chicken bouillon
1 green pepper, deseeded and sliced	1 green pepper, deseeded and sliced
100 g/4 oz button mushrooms, sliced	1 cup sliced button mushrooms
225 g/8 oz cooked chicken, diced	1 cup diced cooked chicken
1 × 113 g/4 oz packet frozen	1 × $\frac{1}{4}$ lb package frozen kernel corn
sweetcorn	salt
salt	freshly ground black pepper
freshly ground black pepper	**To Garnish:**
To Garnish:	tomato slices
tomato slices	

Heat the butter in a large frying pan (skillet). Fry the onion and bacon until golden.

Stir in the rice and cook for 1 minute. Stir in the stock (bouillon). Reserve a few slices of the green pepper for garnish, then chop the remainder and add with the mushrooms to the pan. Bring to the boil. Cover and simmer gently for about 20 minutes until most of the stock (bouillon) has been absorbed.

Stir in the chicken, sweetcorn (kernel corn) and salt and pepper and cook gently for a further 10 to 15 minutes until the stock has been absorbed.

Stir with a fork and turn into a warmed serving dish. Garnish with tomato slices and reserved green pepper rings.

Serves 4

Crunchy Chicken Croquettes

METRIC/IMPERIAL	AMERICAN
40 g/1½ oz butter	3 tablespoons butter
25 g/1 oz mushrooms, washed and finely chopped	¼ cup washed and finely chopped mushrooms
40 g/1½ oz plain flour	6 tablespoons all-purpose flour
1 chicken stock cube	1 chicken bouillon cube
120 ml/4 fl oz milk	½ cup milk
225 g/8 oz cooked chicken, minced	½ lb ground cooked chicken
salt	salt
freshly ground black pepper	freshly ground black pepper
2 teaspoons brown pickle	2 teaspoons brown pickle
1 egg, beaten	1 egg, beaten
75 g/3 oz cornflakes, crushed	¾ cup crushed cornflakes
oil for frying	oil for frying
To Garnish:	**To Garnish:**
sprig of fresh parsley	sprig of fresh parsley

Heat the butter in a saucepan and fry the mushrooms until golden. Stir in the flour and cook for 2 minutes.

Remove from the heat. Add the crumbled chicken stock (bouillon) cube and gradually add the milk, stirring. Return to the heat, bring to the boil, stirring.

Remove from the heat. Add chicken, salt, pepper and pickle. Mix well. Leave to cool.

Roll into 12 cylindrical croquettes on a lightly floured board. Dip into the beaten egg and then into the crushed cornflakes, pressing them on to the surface.

Heat enough oil in a frying pan (skillet) to come halfway up the croquettes. Fry in hot oil for about 5 minutes, turning them frequently until golden brown.

Drain on kitchen paper towels. Arrange on a warmed serving dish and garnish with parsley.

Makes 12 croquettes

Taunton Chicken

METRIC/IMPERIAL	AMERICAN
6 chicken joints	6 chicken joints
25 g/1 oz plain flour	$\frac{1}{4}$ cup all-purpose flour
salt	salt
freshly ground black pepper	freshly ground black pepper
100 g/4 oz butter	1 cup butter
600 ml/1 pint dry cider	$2\frac{1}{2}$ cups dry hard cider
1 small onion	1 small onion
142 ml/5 fl oz carton double cream	$\frac{2}{3}$ cup heavy cream
2 dessert apples	2 dessert apples
To Garnish:	**To Garnish:**
1 tablespoon chopped fresh parsley	1 tablespoon chopped fresh parsley
lemon slices	lemon slices

Coat the chicken joints in the flour, seasoned with salt and pepper. Heat half the butter in a large saucepan and fry the chicken until pale golden.

Stir in the cider, bring to the boil and cook gently. Add the whole onion, cover and simmer for 45 minutes.

Discard the onion. Stir in the cream and cook gently for a few minutes without boiling.

Core and slice the apples but do not peel. Fry gently in the remaining butter, then add to the chicken.

Arrange the chicken on a warmed serving dish and pour the sauce over. Garnish with the parsley and lemon slices and serve hot.
Serves 6

Italian Chicken

METRIC/IMPERIAL	AMERICAN
1.5 kg/$3\frac{1}{2}$ lb roasting chicken	$3\frac{1}{2}$ lb roasting chicken
salt	salt
freshly ground black pepper	freshly ground black pepper
100 g/4 oz salami, cut into strips	$\frac{1}{4}$ lb salami, cut into strips
1 packet minestrone soup	1 package minestrone soup
600 ml/1 pint water	$2\frac{1}{2}$ cups water

Wipe and skin chicken, sprinkle with salt and pepper. Place in a casserole and scatter salami strips over.

Blend the soup mix with the water, bring to the boil, stirring continuously, and pour over the chicken.

Cover and cook in a preheated moderate oven (180°C/350°F, Gas Mark 4) for $1\frac{3}{4}$ hours until tender. Serve hot with buttered spaghetti.
Serves 4 to 6

TAUNTON CHICKEN (*Photograph: Taunton Cider*)

Turkey Suprême

METRIC/IMPERIAL	AMERICAN
25 g/1 oz butter	2 tablespoons butter
75 g/3 oz mushrooms, sliced	1 cup sliced mushrooms
1 small onion, chopped	1 small onion, chopped
25 g/1 oz flour	$\frac{1}{4}$ cup flour
300 ml/10 fl oz chicken stock	$1\frac{1}{4}$ cups chicken bouillon
2 teaspoons lemon juice	2 teaspoons lemon juice
500 g/1 lb cooked turkey, chopped	1 lb cooked turkey, chopped
225 g/8 oz long-grain rice	1 cup long grain rice
1 egg yolk	1 egg yolk
50 ml/2 fl oz double cream	$\frac{1}{4}$ cup heavy cream
salt	salt
freshly ground black pepper	freshly ground black pepper
To Garnish:	**To Garnish:**
2 tablespoons chopped fresh parsley	2 tablespoons chopped fresh parsley

Melt the butter in a saucepan. Add the mushrooms and onion and fry for 5 minutes. Stir in the flour to form a smooth paste. Gradually stir in the chicken stock (bouillon). Bring to the boil, then simmer for 2 minutes stirring continually. Stir in the lemon juice and turkey and cook the sauce for 30 minutes.

Meanwhile, cook the rice in boiling, salted water for 15 to 20 minutes, or until the rice is tender and the liquid is absorbed. Transfer the rice to a warmed serving dish and keep hot.

Mix the egg yolk, cream, salt and pepper together, then stir in 3 tablespoons of the sauce. Gradually stir into the sauce and cook gently for 2 minutes without bringing to the boil. Spoon the sauce over the rice and garnish with the parsley.

Serves 4

Turkey Stuffed Peppers

METRIC/IMPERIAL

2 green peppers
2 red peppers
1 tablespoon oil
50 g/2 oz streaky bacon, derinded
  and chopped
1 onion, chopped
1 clove garlic, crushed
50 g/2 oz mushrooms, chopped
1 tablespoon chopped fresh parsley
salt
freshly ground black pepper
350 g/12 oz cooked turkey, cubed
25 g/1 oz cheese, grated

AMERICAN

2 green peppers
2 red peppers
1 tablespoon oil
3 fatty bacon slices, derinded and
  chopped
1 onion, chopped
1 clove garlic, crushed
$\frac{1}{2}$ cup chopped mushrooms
1 tablespoon chopped fresh parsley
salt
freshly ground black pepper
$\frac{3}{4}$ lb cooked cubed turkey
$\frac{1}{4}$ cup grated cheese

Slice the tops off the peppers and remove the seeds and membranes.
Blanch the peppers and tops in boiling salted water for 5 minutes. Rinse
in cold water and drain thoroughly. Chop the tops of the peppers.

Heat the oil in a saucepan and fry bacon, onion, garlic and
mushrooms for 5 minutes. Add parsley, salt and pepper, chopped
peppers and cubed turkey. Mix well.

Pile mixture into pepper shells and stand them upright in a casserole.
Top with the grated cheese and cover with a lid or foil.

Bake in a moderate oven (180°C/350°F, Gas Mark 4) for 20 minutes.
Uncover and cook for a further 10 minutes until tender.

Arrange on a warmed serving dish and serve hot.

Serves 4

Turkey Cobbler

METRIC/IMPERIAL
2 × 275 g/10 oz turkey thighs
2 tablespoons oil
1 large onion, sliced
1 tablespoon plain flour
150 ml/$\frac{1}{4}$ pint turkey stock
1 × 400 g/14 oz can tomatoes
$\frac{1}{4}$ teaspoon Tabasco sauce
salt
freshly ground black pepper
1 × 325 g/11$\frac{1}{2}$ oz can sweetcorn
  kernels
200 g/7 oz self-raising flour
50 g/2 oz butter or margarine
2 tablespoons chopped fresh parsley
142 ml/5 fl oz carton soured cream

AMERICAN
2 × 10 oz turkey thighs
2 tablespoons oil
1 large onion, sliced
1 tablespoon all-purpose flour
$\frac{2}{3}$ cup turkey bouillon
1 × 14 oz can tomatoes
$\frac{1}{4}$ teaspoon Tabasco sauce
salt
freshly ground black pepper
1 × 11$\frac{1}{2}$ oz can kernel corn
1$\frac{3}{4}$ cups self-rising flour
$\frac{1}{4}$ cup butter or margarine
2 tablespoons chopped fresh parsley
$\frac{2}{3}$ cup sour cream

Bone the turkey thighs, remove skin and discard. Heat the oil in a heavy saucepan and fry the meat until golden.

Add the onion and fry gently for a few minutes, stirring. Stir in the flour and cook for 2 minutes. Gradually add the stock (bouillon), tomatoes with their juice, Tabasco, salt and pepper. Bring to the boil, stirring continuously. Cover and simmer for 25 minutes.

Add the drained corn. Pour into a 1.75 litre/3 pint/7$\frac{1}{2}$ cup dish.

Sift the flour with a pinch of salt. Rub in the butter or margarine and stir in the parsley and soured cream. Knead lightly to bind, then roll out to about 1 cm/$\frac{1}{2}$ in thickness and with a 6.5 cm/2$\frac{1}{2}$ in fluted round cutter, stamp out 12 rounds.

Arrange in an overlapping circle on the turkey mixture. Bake in a preheated hot oven (220°C/425°F, Gas Mark 7) for about 20 minutes until cobblers are well risen and golden. Serve hot.

Serves 4

TURKEY COBBLER (*Photograph: British Turkey Federation*)

Chicken Curry

METRIC/IMPERIAL

25 g/1 oz butter or margarine
1 onion, chopped
1 clove garlic, crushed
1 green pepper, deseeded and chopped
15 g/½ oz plain flour
2 tablespoons curry powder
¼ teaspoon paprika
¼ teaspoon cayenne
450 ml/¾ pint chicken stock
1 cooking apple, peeled, cored and
  chopped
2 tablespoons lemon juice
salt
freshly ground black pepper
500 g/1 lb cooked chicken, sliced
500 g/1 lb fresh beansprouts

AMERICAN

2 tablespoons butter or margarine
1 onion, chopped
1 clove garlic, crushed
1 green pepper, deseeded and chopped
2 tablespoons all-purpose flour
2 tablespoons curry powder
¼ teaspoon paprika
¼ teaspoon cayenne
2 cups chicken bouillon
1 baking apple, peeled, cored and
  chopped
2 tablespoons lemon juice
salt
freshly ground black pepper
1 lb cooked chicken, sliced
1 lb fresh beansprouts

Heat the butter or margarine in a large saucepan. Fry the onion, garlic and pepper for 2 to 3 minutes.

Stir in the flour and spices and cook for a further 2 minutes. Gradually stir in the stock (bouillon). Add the apple, lemon juice, salt and pepper and bring to the boil, stirring. Cover and simmer gently for 45 minutes, stirring occasionally. Add the chicken and cook for a further 15 minutes.

Cook the beansprouts in boiling water for 1 minute. Drain thoroughly and arrange in a border round a warmed serving dish. Arrange the curry in the centre and serve hot with an apple, cucumber and yogurt salad.

Serves 4

Roast Chicken with Golden Stuffing

METRIC/IMPERIAL
1.5 kg/3 lb roasting chicken with
 giblets
75 g/3 oz butter
1 onion, chopped
50 g/2 oz streaky bacon, derinded
 and chopped
2 sticks celery, chopped
100 g/4 oz long-grain rice
300 ml/½ pint chicken stock
25 g/1 oz walnuts, chopped
25 g/1 oz sultanas
salt
freshly ground black pepper
To Garnish:
few sprigs of watercress

AMERICAN
3 lb roasting chicken with giblets
¾ cup butter
1 onion, chopped
3 fatty bacon slices, derinded and
 chopped
2 stalks celery, chopped
¾ cup long-grain rice
1¼ cups chicken bouillon
¼ cup chopped walnuts
¼ cup seedless white raisins
salt
freshly ground black pepper
To Garnish:
few sprigs of watercress

Wipe the chicken. Heat 25 g/1 oz/2 tablespoons of butter in a saucepan. Fry the chopped chicken liver, onion, bacon, celery and rice for 3 minutes.

Add the stock (bouillon), made from the remaining giblets, and cook over a low heat for 15 minutes, stirring occasionally until the stock is absorbed.

Add the walnuts and sultanas (raisins) and salt and pepper to taste. Stuff chicken with the rice mixture and place in a roasting tin. Spread the remaining butter over the chicken. Cover with foil. Roast in a moderately hot oven (200°C/400°F, Gas Mark 6) for 1 hour. Uncover and cook for a further 30 minutes.

Place on a warmed serving dish, garnish with watercress and serve hot.

Serves 4 to 6

Creamy Chicken Pastry

METRIC/IMPERIAL

750 g/1½ lb chicken joints
600 ml/1 pint chicken stock
1 bay leaf
¼ teaspoon dried rosemary
salt
freshly ground black pepper
500 g/1 lb puff pastry
1 egg
225 g/8 oz button mushrooms,
    washed and dried
1 small green pepper, skinned,
    deseeded and chopped
65 g/2½ oz butter
50 g/2 oz plain flour
300 ml/½ pint milk

AMERICAN

1½ lb chicken joints
2½ cups chicken bouillon
1 bay leaf
¼ teaspoon dried rosemary
salt
freshly ground black pepper
1 lb puff pastry
1 egg
2 cups button mushrooms, washed
    and dried
1 small green pepper, skinned,
    deseeded and chopped
½ cup butter
½ cup all-purpose flour
1¼ cups milk

Place the chicken pieces in a pan with the chicken stock (bouillon); add the bay leaf and the rosemary, and salt and pepper. Simmer for about 45 minutes until the chicken is tender.

Roll out pastry to make 2 × 20 cm/8 in squares. Place one on a baking sheet and brush with beaten egg. Cover with the second square and at the centre mark a 2.5 cm/1 in square with a sharp knife. Score a lattice pattern within the square. Brush with egg and bake in a preheated hot oven (220°C/425°F, Gas Mark 7) for 25 minutes. Remove centre square and reserve. Lift out soft pastry from the centre of the case and discard. Reduce oven to moderate (160°C/325°F, Gas Mark 3) and return case to oven for 10 minutes.

Remove chicken pieces and bay leaf from pan and boil stock (bouillon) down to 300 ml/½ pint/1¼ cups.

Remove the bones from the chicken and cut it into 1 cm/½ in cubes. Reserve a few of the mushrooms for garnish and quarter the rest. Heat 40 g/1½ oz/3 tablespoons of the butter in a saucepan and cook both lots of mushrooms. Remove from the pan. Add the remaining butter and chopped pepper. Cook for 2 minutes, then stir in the flour and gradually blend in the milk and chicken stock (bouillon). Bring to the boil, stirring continuously. Add the quartered mushrooms and chicken. Adjust seasoning and heat thoroughly.

Place the pastry case on a warmed serving dish, fill with chicken mixture, top with the pastry lid and garnish with the whole mushrooms. Serve hot.

Serves 4 to 6

CREAMY CHICKEN PASTRY (Photographer: Paul Williams)

BUDGET MEALS

Festival Fish Pie

METRIC/IMPERIAL	AMERICAN
350 g/12 oz smoked haddock	$\frac{3}{4}$ lb smoked haddock
150 ml/$\frac{1}{4}$ pint milk	$\frac{2}{3}$ cup milk
25 g/1 oz butter or margarine	2 tablespoons butter or margarine
25 g/1 oz plain flour	$\frac{1}{4}$ cup all-purpose flour
2 tablespoons chopped fresh parsley	2 tablespoons chopped fresh parsley
salt	salt
freshly ground black pepper	freshly ground black pepper
1 × 212 g/7$\frac{1}{2}$ oz packet frozen puff pastry, thawed	1 × 7$\frac{1}{2}$ oz package frozen puff pastry, thawed
1 egg, beaten	1 egg, beaten

Place haddock in a frying pan (skillet). Add the milk, cover and bring to the boil. Simmer for 10 minutes.

Reserve liquid for sauce and make up to 150 ml/$\frac{1}{4}$ pint/$\frac{2}{3}$ cup. Skin fish, flake roughly and remove any bones.

Melt the butter or margarine in a saucepan, add the flour and cook for 2 minutes. Gradually add the reserved liquid. Bring to the boil, stirring continuously until sauce is thick and smooth. Add the fish, parsley and salt and pepper to taste. Allow to cool.

Roll out the pastry thinly to a large square and place on a baking sheet. Put the filling in the centre, brush the edges of pastry with beaten egg and draw the corners up to the middle to form an envelope shape. Pinch edges well together to seal.

Brush the pie with beaten egg and bake near the top of a preheated hot oven (220°C/425°F, Gas Mark 7) for 30 minutes until golden. Serve hot with fresh vegetables.

Serves 4

Tuna Fish and Peanut Risotto

METRIC/IMPERIAL

225 g/8 oz long-grain rice
2 × 198 g/7 oz cans tuna fish
4 tablespoons oil
2 onions, chopped
1 green pepper, halved, deseeded and sliced
2 teaspoons curry powder
200 g/7 oz salted peanuts
450 ml/¾ pint apple juice or cider
salt
freshly ground black pepper
100 g/4 oz cooking apple, diced
2 tablespoons lemon juice
3 tablespoons sugar

AMERICAN

1 cup long-grain rice
2 × 7 oz cans tuna fish
4 tablespoons oil
2 onions, chopped
1 green pepper, halved, deseeded and sliced
2 teaspoons curry powder
1 cup salted peanuts
2 cups apple juice or hard cider
salt
freshly ground black pepper
1 cup diced baking apple
2 tablespoons lemon juice
3 tablespoons sugar

Cook the rice in a pan of boiling salted water for 10 minutes and drain thoroughly. Drain the tuna fish and cut into large chunks.

Heat the oil in a large saucepan and fry the onion and green pepper with the curry powder for 5 minutes. Grind the peanuts in a food mill or blender and add to the pan with the apple juice or cider, salt, pepper, diced apple, lemon juice and sugar. Bring to the boil and add the rice and tuna fish.

Simmer, uncovered, for 10 minutes, stirring frequently. Adjust the seasoning, transfer to a warmed serving dish and serve hot with pickled red cabbage.

Serves 6

Gruyère Soufflé

METRIC/IMPERIAL	AMERICAN
450 ml/¾ pint milk	2 cups milk
6 tablespoons water	6 tablespoons water
4 tablespoons semolina	¼ cup semolina
40 g/1½ oz butter	3 tablespoons butter
175 g/6 oz Gruyère cheese, grated	1½ cups grated Gruyère cheese
salt	salt
white pepper	white pepper
pinch of grated nutmeg	pinch of grated nutmeg
4 eggs, separated	4 eggs, separated

Heat the milk and water in a large saucepan. Sprinkle in the semolina and bring to the boil, stirring. Boil for 3 minutes, stirring continuously. Add the butter and stir until it melts.

Remove the pan from the heat and stir in the cheese. Stir until the cheese has melted. Add salt and pepper and nutmeg and leave to cool.

Grease a 1.25 litre/2¼ pint/5¾ cup soufflé dish. Beat the egg yolks until liquid. Whisk the egg whites with a pinch of salt until stiff but not dry.

Beat the egg yolks into the semolina and cheese mixture. Stir in 1 tablespoon of the egg whites. Gently fold in the remaining whites.

Bake in a preheated moderately hot oven (190°C/375°F, Gas Mark 5) for 40 to 50 minutes or until the soufflé is risen and browned on top.

Remove the dish from the oven and serve the soufflé immediately.

Serves 4

Stuffed Potatoes

METRIC/IMPERIAL	AMERICAN
4 potatoes, baked and halved	4 potatoes, baked and halved
25 g/1 oz butter	2 tablespoons butter
3 eggs, separated	3 eggs, separated
50 g/2 oz cooked ham, diced	¼ cup diced cooked ham
salt	salt
freshly ground black pepper	freshly ground black pepper
50 g/2 oz Parmesan cheese, grated	½ cup grated Parmesan cheese

Scoop the pulp out of the potatoes and mash well. Mix in the butter, egg yolks and ham. Press the mixture back into the potato halves. Beat the egg whites until they are stiff, fold in the cheese and salt and pepper to taste.

Put the potatoes on a baking sheet and pile the mixture on top. Put into a preheated, moderate oven (160°C/325°F, Gas Mark 3) and bake for 10 minutes.

Serves 4

GRUYERE SOUFFLE (*Photograph: Cheeses from Switzerland Ltd*)

Sardine Quiche

METRIC/IMPERIAL

Pastry:
175 g/6 oz plain flour
pinch of salt
75 g/3 oz butter or margarine

Filling:
15 g/$\frac{1}{2}$ oz butter or margarine
1 onion, chopped
50 g/2 oz mushrooms, sliced
1 × 120 g/$4\frac{1}{4}$ oz can sardines, drained
  and halved lengthways
2 eggs
150 ml/$\frac{1}{4}$ pint milk
75 g/3 oz cheese, grated
salt
freshly ground black pepper

AMERICAN

Pastry:
1$\frac{1}{2}$ cups all-purpose flour
pinch of salt
6 tablespoons butter or margarine

Filling:
1 tablespoon butter or margarine
1 onion, chopped
$\frac{1}{2}$ cup sliced mushrooms
1 × $4\frac{1}{4}$ oz can sardines, drained and
  halved lengthways
2 eggs
$\frac{2}{3}$ cup milk
$\frac{3}{4}$ cup grated cheese
salt
freshly ground black pepper

To make the pastry, sift the flour and salt into a bowl, rub in the fat until the mixture resembles fine breadcrumbs. Add enough water to mix to a stiff paste. Knead on a lightly floured surface until smooth. Roll out and use to line a 20 cm/8 in flan dish (pie dish).

To make the filling, heat the fat in a frying pan (skillet) and fry the onion and mushrooms for 3 to 4 minutes. Cool slightly then spread over pastry. Arrange half the sardine halves in the flan (pie).

Whisk together the eggs and milk, add the cheese and salt and pepper and pour into the pastry case. Arrange remaining halved sardines on top. Bake in a preheated moderately hot oven (200°C/400°F, Gas Mark 6) for 15 minutes. Reduce heat to moderate (180°C/350°F, Gas Mark 4) for a further 10 to 15 minutes. Serve hot or cold with a salad.
Serves 4

Danish Vegetable Crumble

METRIC/IMPERIAL
100 g/4 oz butter
175 g/6 oz plain flour
75 g/3 oz Danish blue cheese, grated
freshly ground black pepper
2 onions, sliced
4 sticks celery, sliced
175 g/6 oz carrots, sliced
450 ml/¾ pint water
1 tablespoon yeast extract
500 g/1 lb cabbage, shredded
225 g/8 oz tomatoes, skinned and
  chopped
salt
To Garnish:
sprigs of fresh parsley

AMERICAN
½ cup butter
1½ cups all-purpose flour
¾ cup grated Danish blue cheese
freshly ground black pepper
2 onions, sliced
4 sticks celery, sliced
1 cup sliced carrot
2 cups water
1 tablespoon yeast extract
6 cups shredded cabbage
1 cup skinned and chopped tomatoes
salt
To Garnish:
sprigs of fresh parsley

Rub half the butter into 150 g/5 oz/1¼ cups of the flour and stir in the grated cheese. Add a little pepper and reserve.

Heat the remaining butter in a saucepan and fry the onions, celery and carrots for 10 minutes until golden. Stir in the remaining flour and gradually add the water. Bring to the boil, stirring continuously. Stir in the yeast extract.

Add the cabbage and tomatoes, salt and pepper. Place in a 2.25 litre/4 pint/10 cup casserole. Spread crumble mixture evenly over the vegetables. Bake in a preheated moderate oven (180°C/350°F, Gas Mark 4) for 1 hour. Garnish with the parsley and serve hot.
Serves 4

Grecian Hotpot

METRIC/IMPERIAL	AMERICAN
2 tablespoons oil	2 tablespoons oil
2 onions, cut into wedges	2 onions, cut into wedges
2 sticks celery, sliced	2 stalks celery, sliced
100 g/4 oz runner beans, sliced	$\frac{1}{2}$ cup sliced French beans
300 ml/$\frac{1}{2}$ pint beef stock	1$\frac{1}{4}$ cups beef bouillon
2 tablespoons tomato ketchup	2 tablespoons tomato catsup
freshly ground black pepper	freshly ground black pepper
100 g/4 oz salted peanuts	$\frac{1}{2}$ cup salted peanuts
1 × 340 g/12 oz can corned beef, chopped	1 × 12 oz can corned beef, chopped

Heat the oil in a saucepan. Add the onion and celery, fry for 10 minutes. Add the beans and stock (bouillon), simmer for 15 minutes. Add the ketchup (catsup) and pepper to taste.

Chop half the peanuts finely. Add the meat to the pan with the chopped peanuts; simmer for 5 minutes. Adjust seasoning.

Transfer to a warmed serving dish and sprinkle whole peanuts over.

Serves 4

Pork 'n Pasta

METRIC/IMPERIAL	AMERICAN
225 g/8 oz spaghetti	$\frac{1}{2}$ lb spaghetti
2 tablespoons oil	2 tablespoons oil
1 large onion, chopped	1 large onion, chopped
100 g/4 oz mushrooms, sliced	1 cup sliced mushrooms
1 × 400 g/14 oz can tomatoes	1 × 14 oz can tomatoes
2 tablespoons tomato purée	2 tablespoons tomato paste
$\frac{1}{2}$ teaspoon dried mixed herbs	$\frac{1}{2}$ teaspoon dried mixed herbs
1 × 500 g/1 lb can chopped ham and pork, diced	1 lb can chopped pork and ham, diced
salt	salt
freshly ground black pepper	freshly ground black pepper
2 tablespoons Parmesan cheese, grated	2 tablespoons grated Parmesan cheese

Boil the spaghetti in salted water for 10 minutes until *al dente*.

Meanwhile, heat the oil in a saucepan and fry the onion until golden; add mushrooms, tomatoes, tomato purée (paste) and herbs. Add the meat and salt and pepper to taste. Simmer gently for 10 minutes.

Drain the spaghetti and arrange on a warmed serving dish. Arrange the tomato mixture along the centre, sprinkle with Parmesan cheese and serve hot with a tossed green salad.

Serves 4

(Photograph: African Groundnut Council Information Service)

Storecupboard Moussaka

METRIC/IMPERIAL	AMERICAN
2 aubergines	2 eggplants
salt	salt
6 tablespoons oil	6 tablespoons oil
1 large onion, chopped	1 large onion, chopped
1 clove garlic, crushed	1 clove garlic, crushed
100 g/4 oz mushrooms, sliced	1 cup sliced mushrooms
2 tablespoons tomato purée	2 tablespoons tomato paste
1 × 447 g/15¾ oz can soya mince or savoury mince	1 × 15¾ oz can soya mince or savoury mince
freshly ground black pepper	freshly ground black pepper
25 g/1 oz butter	2 tablespoons butter
25 g/1 oz plain flour	¼ cup all-purpose flour
300 ml/½ pint milk	1¼ cups milk
75 g/3 oz cheese, grated	¾ cup grated cheese

Wash the aubergines (eggplants) and remove the stalks. Cut into 0.5 cm/¼ in thick slices. Place on a large plate and sprinkle with salt. Leave for 45 minutes, then drain, rinse and dry well.

Fry the aubergines (eggplants) on both sides in half the oil, until pale gold in colour. Drain. Fry the onion in the remaining oil, add the garlic and cook until soft. Stir in the mushrooms, tomato purée (paste) and soya or savoury mince; add salt and pepper and simmer for 3 minutes.

Line a dish with half the aubergines (eggplants), top with the mince mixture, then cover with the rest of the aubergine (eggplant) slices.

Melt the butter in a small saucepan, stir in the flour and cook for 2 minutes, stirring continuously. Gradually add the milk and bring to the boil, stirring continuously. Remove from the heat, stir in the cheese and add salt and pepper to taste. Pour over the aubergine (eggplant) slices, covering them completely.

Bake in a preheated moderate oven (180°C/350°F, Gas Mark 4) for 30 to 40 minutes until golden brown. Serve hot with a tomato and onion salad.

Serves 4

DESSERTS AND PUDDINGS

Golden Fruit Flan

METRIC/IMPERIAL
1 × 375 g/13 oz packet frozen puff
  pastry, thawed
4 dessert apples
1 × 312 g/11 oz can mandarin
  oranges
2 tablespoons caster sugar
50 g/2 oz apricot jam
2 tablespoons lemon juice
1 egg, beaten

AMERICAN
13 oz package frozen puff pastry,
  thawed
4 dessert apples
11 oz can mandarin oranges
2 tablespoons sugar
4 tablespoons apricot jam
2 tablespoons lemon juice
1 egg, beaten

Roll out the pastry into a rectangle 30 cm × 20 cm/12 in × 8 in and trim neatly. Cut a strip 1 cm/$\frac{1}{2}$ in wide from each side. Place the pastry rectangle on a greased baking sheet and brush the border with water. Place the strips on top to form a raised border and neaten the corners. Knock up the outside edges with the back of a knife and flute. Mark the top of the border decoratively. Prick the base of the flan (pie) with a fork.

Peel, core, quarter and slice the apples thinly. Arrange overlapping slices of apple in 4 rows across the flan (pie), leaving a 2.5 cm/1 in gap between each row. Sprinkle fruit with sugar and bake the flan (pie) in a preheated hot oven (220°C/425°F, Gas Mark 7) for 15 minutes until the pastry is well risen and golden brown.

Remove from the oven and leave to cool. Drain the mandarin oranges and arrange between apples.

Melt the jam in a small saucepan with the lemon juice. Bring to the boil, stirring. Allow to cool slightly and spoon carefully over the fruit. Spoon a little of the glaze over the top and outside of the pastry border. Serve cold with whipped cream.

Serves 6 to 8

Fruit Roly Poly

METRIC/IMPERIAL	AMERICAN
225 g/8 oz self-raising flour	*2 cups self-rising flour*
½ teaspoon salt	*½ teaspoon salt*
1 teaspoon baking powder	*1 teaspoon baking powder*
100 g/4 oz beef suet, finely chopped	*⅔ cup finely chopped beef suet*
150 ml/¼ pint water	*⅔ cup water*
1 tablespoon orange marmalade	*1 tablespoon orange marmalade*
100 g/4 oz dried mixed fruit	*⅔ cup dried mixed fruit*
Sauce:	**Sauce:**
6 tablespoons golden syrup	*6 tablespoons maple syrup*
2 tablespoons lemon juice	*2 tablespoons lemon juice*

Lightly brush a fairly large sheet of greaseproof paper with oil. Sift the flour, salt and baking powder together and stir in the suet. Add the water to form a soft dough. Knead the mixture lightly and roll out on a lightly floured surface to 1 cm/½ in thick.

Spread the dough with the marmalade and sprinkle the dried fruit over. Roll up neatly, wrap in the greaseproof paper, making a pleat in the paper to allow the pudding to expand. Wrap loosely in foil and seal the ends well.

Place the pudding in a saucepan and add boiling water to come half way up the roll. Cover and simmer for 1½ hours, adding more water when necessary.

Heat the syrup and lemon juice together. Remove the pudding from the wrappings, place on a warmed serving dish and serve in slices with the sauce poured over.

Serves 6

FRUIT ROLY POLY *(Photograph: British Sugar Bureau)*

Brown Bread Pudding

METRIC/IMPERIAL	AMERICAN
500 g/1 lb fresh brown or wholemeal bread	1 lb fresh brown or wholemeal bread
150 ml/¼ pint Guinness	⅔ cup Guinness
75 g/3 oz raisins	½ cup raisins
75 g/3 oz sultanas	½ cup seedless white raisins
75 g/3 oz finely chopped suet	½ cup finely chopped suet
½ teaspoon mixed spice	½ teaspoon mixed spice
7 tablespoons caster sugar	7 tablespoons sugar
1 egg, beaten	1 egg, beaten

Break the bread into small pieces and place in a large bowl. Cover with the Guinness and leave to soak for at least 30 minutes. Add the dried fruit, suet, spice, all but 1 tablespoon sugar and the egg.

Mix well and place in a greased 18 cm/7 in round ovenproof dish. Bake in a preheated moderate oven (160°C/325°F, Gas Mark 3) for 1 hour until firm and springy to the touch.

Dredge with the remaining sugar and serve hot with custard sauce.
Serves 6

Honeyed Baked Apple

METRIC/IMPERIAL	AMERICAN
4 medium cooking apples	4 medium baking apples
50 g/2 oz sultanas	½ cup white seedless raisins
50 g/2 oz mixed peel	½ cup chopped mixed peel
25 g/1 oz chopped walnuts	¼ cup chopped walnuts
4 tablespoons clear honey	4 tablespoons clear honey
6 tablespoons water	6 tablespoons water

Wipe the apples with a damp cloth and remove the cores, making a fairly large cavity. Slit the skins around the centre to prevent them bursting during cooking.

Mix together the sultanas, peel and chopped walnuts with half the honey to bind. Stuff the apples with the filling and place in a buttered ovenproof dish. Add the water and spoon remaining honey over. Cover with buttered greaseproof paper and bake in a preheated moderate oven (180°C/350°F, Gas Mark 4).

Remove the apples from the oven. Arrange on a warmed serving dish, and baste with honey liquid. Serve hot with cream, if liked.
Serves 4

Apple and Marmalade Flan

METRIC/IMPERIAL

Pastry:

100 g/4 oz plain flour
50 g/2 oz cornflour
75 g/3 oz butter
25 g/1 oz caster sugar
1 egg

Filling:

4 tablespoons fine cut marmalade
500 g/1 lb cooking apples, peeled,
  cored and sliced
2 tablespoons demerara sugar

Topping:

1 tablespoon caster sugar
1 × 142 ml/5 fl oz carton double
  cream
1 tablespoon brandy or sherry

AMERICAN

Pastry:

1 cup all-purpose flour
½ cup cornstarch
6 tablespoons butter
2 tablespoons sugar
1 egg

Filling:

4 tablespoons fine cut marmalade
1 lb baking apples, peeled, cored and
  sliced
2 tablespoons brown sugar

Topping:

1 tablespoon sugar
⅔ cup heavy cream
1 tablespoon brandy or sherry

To make the pastry, sift the flour and cornflour (cornstarch) into a large bowl and rub in the butter until the mixture resembles fine breadcrumbs. Stir in the sugar and the egg and mix to a smooth dough. Roll out half the pastry and use to line an 18 cm/7 in flan tin (pie pan).

Spread the marmalade over the base of the pastry case and arrange the apples on top. Sprinkle with the demerara sugar.

Roll out the remaining pastry and use to cover the flan. Make three cuts in the centre to form a six-point star. Turn back each centre point to expose the filling. Bake in a preheated moderately hot oven (200°C/400°F, Gas Mark 6) for 35 to 40 minutes. Sprinkle with sugar and allow to cool.

Whip the cream until stiff and fold in the brandy or sherry. Pile the cream in the centre of the cold flan and serve.

Serves 6

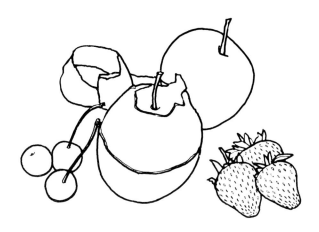

Fruit Sorbet

METRIC/IMPERIAL	AMERICAN
450 ml/¾ pint fruit juice – orange, grapefruit, pineapple etc	2 cups fruit juice – orange, grapefruit, pineapple etc
2 tablespoons water	2 tablespoons water
15 g/½ oz gelatine	1 tablespoon gelatin
50 g/2 oz caster sugar	¼ cup sugar
2 egg whites	2 egg whites
To Decorate:	**To Decorate:**
fruit, wafers and whipped cream (optional)	fruit, wafers and whipped cream (optional)

Chill the fruit juice. Sprinkle the gelatine into 2 tablespoons water in a bowl. Stand the bowl in a pan of simmering water and stir until dissolved

Stir the sugar into the gelatine mixture and stir until dissolved. Add the fruit juice, mix well and pour into a freezer tray. Freeze until mushy.

Whisk the egg whites to soft peaks and fold into the fruit ice. Return to the freezer tray and freeze until firm.

Place in the refrigerator for 10 minutes before serving. Scoop into individual glasses and decorate with fruit, wafers and whipped cream.
Serves 4

Pots de Crème

METRIC/IMPERIAL	AMERICAN
4 eggs	4 eggs
25 g/1 oz caster sugar	¼ cup sugar
600 ml/1 pint milk	2½ cups milk
6 tablespoons double cream	6 tablespoons heavy cream
To Decorate:	**To Decorate:**
25 g/1 oz flaked almonds, toasted chocolate curls	¼ cup slivered almonds, toasted chocolate curls

Beat the eggs with the sugar until frothy. Heat the milk almost to boiling point and whisk into the eggs. Strain into 4 individual dishes, standing in a roasting tin containing enough water to come half-way up the dishes. Bake in a preheated moderate oven (160°C/325°F, Gas Mark 3) for 25 to 30 minutes until set.

Remove the dishes from the tin and allow to cool. Whip the cream and pipe a whirl on to each custard. Decorate with the almonds and chocolate curls and chill before serving.
Serves 4

FRUIT SORBET (Photograph: British Egg Information Service)

Chocolate Meringue Pie

METRIC/IMPERIAL
175 g/6 oz shortcrust pastry
300 ml/½ pint evaporated milk
150 ml/¼ pint water
50 g/2 oz cornflour
40 g/1½ oz drinking chocolate
pinch of ground cinnamon
2 eggs, separated
100 g/4 oz caster sugar

AMERICAN
6 oz basic pie dough made with
  all-purpose flour
1¼ cups evaporated milk
⅔ cup water
½ cup cornstarch
3 tablespoons drinking chocolate
pinch of ground cinnamon
2 eggs, separated
½ cup sugar

Roll out the pastry and use to line a 20 cm/8 in flan tin (pie pan). Bake blind and allow to cool.

To make the filling, mix the evaporated milk with the water in a saucepan. Blend in the cornflour (cornstarch), then add the drinking chocolate and cinnamon. Bring to the boil, stirring continuously. Cook for 3 minutes. Cool slightly. Separate the eggs and beat the egg yolks into the chocolate filling. Pour the filling into the baked pastry case.

Whisk the egg whites until stiff. Whisk in half the sugar, fold in the rest with a metal spoon. Spoon or pipe the meringue on top of the chocolate filling.

Bake in a preheated hot oven (220°C/425°F, Gas Mark 7) for 10 to 15 minutes until golden. Serve hot or cold.
Serves 6

Minted Fruit Salad

METRIC/IMPERIAL
75 g/3 oz sugar
300 ml/½ pint water
juice of 1 lemon
2 red-skinned apples, cored and sliced
2 oranges, divided into segments
2 pears, cored and sliced
2 bananas, sliced
100 g/4 oz seedless grapes
1 small honeydew melon, cubed
1 tablespoon chopped fresh mint

AMERICAN
6 tablespoons sugar
1¼ cups water
juice of 1 lemon
2 red-skinned apples, cored and sliced
2 oranges, divided into segments
2 pears, cored and sliced
2 bananas, sliced
1 cup seedless grapes
1 small honeydew melon, cubed
1 tablespoon chopped fresh mint

Prepare a syrup by dissolving the sugar in the water over a low heat. Leave to cool. Add the lemon juice and pour into a shallow dish.

Add the prepared fruits. Chop the fresh mint very finely and stir into the syrup. Leave for at least 2 hours before serving with pouring cream.
Serves 6 to 8

Victoria Fruit Trifle

METRIC/IMPERIAL
100 g/4 oz sugar
300 ml/½ pint water
1 cinnamon stick
3 pears
3 dessert apples
4 tablespoons sherry
100 g/4 oz trifle sponges
3 tablespoons raspberry jam
50 g/2 oz ratafia biscuits
600 ml/1 pint thick custard
1 × 142 ml/5 fl oz carton double
  cream
To Decorate:
red apple slices and angelica

AMERICAN
½ cup sugar
1¼ cups water
1 cinnamon stick
3 pears
3 dessert apples
4 tablespoons sherry
¼ lb ladyfingers
3 tablespoons raspberry jam
2 oz ratafia biscuits
2½ cups thick custard
⅔ cup heavy cream
To Decorate:
red apple slices and angelica

Dissolve the sugar in the water in a large pan and add the cinnamon stick.

Peel, core and slice the pears and apples and add to the simmering syrup. Cook gently for 10 minutes until just tender. Carefully drain the slices. Strain off 300 ml/½ pint/1¼ cups of syrup and add the sherry.

Split the sponges (ladyfingers) and spread with the jam. Arrange a layer in the bottom of a glass dish, with a third of the ratafias, and soak with sherry syrup. Top with a layer of sliced fruit. Repeat with a second layer of sponges (ladyfingers) and half the remaining ratafias, and top with remaining fruit. Leave to soak for 30 minutes.

Pour the custard over and chill until set.

Whip the cream and swirl or pipe over the custard and decorate with the reserved ratafia biscuits, angelica and slices of apple.
Serves 4 to 6

Apple Berry Roll-ups

METRIC/IMPERIAL
2 dessert apples, peeled, cored and
  sliced
1 tablespoon water
2 tablespoons sugar
225 g/8 oz raspberries
300 ml/½ pint pancake batter

AMERICAN
2 dessert apples, peeled, cored and
  sliced
1 tablespoon water
2 tablespoons sugar
½ lb raspberries
1¼ cups pancake batter

Cook the apples with the water and sugar for 10 minutes until tender
but not mushy. Add the raspberries and heat through gently.

Cook 8 pancakes in the usual way, keeping them hot until all are
cooked. Divide the apple mixture between the pancakes and roll up.
Place on a warmed serving dish and serve immediately.
Serves 4

Pineapple and Walnut Ice Cream Crunch

METRIC/IMPERIAL
75 g/3 oz butter
225 g/8 oz digestive biscuits, crushed
1 × 15 g/½ oz packet instant
  pineapple drink
300 g/½ pint cold water
1 egg
1 small can evaporated milk, chilled
25 g/1 oz walnuts, chopped

AMERICAN
6 tablespoons butter
3 cups crushed Graham crackers
1 package instant pineapple drink
1¼ cups cold water
1 egg
⅔ cup chilled evaporated milk
¼ cup walnuts, chopped

Melt the butter in a saucepan and add the biscuits. Mix thoroughly.
Stand an 18 cm/7 in flan ring (pie ring) on a baking tray. Press crumbs
evenly over base and up sides. Chill in the refrigerator until firm.

Whisk pineapple drink, water and egg together in a saucepan. Cook
over a low heat, stirring continuously until custard thickens. Strain and
leave until cold.

Whisk evaporated milk until thick and fold it into custard. Pour into
freezing trays and freeze until mushy. Stir in the walnuts and return to
the freezer until firm.

Remove flan (pie) ring from refrigerator, gently lift off ring and
transfer case to the serving plate. Fill with spoonfuls of ice cream and
serve immediately.
Serves 6

APPLE BERRY ROLL-UPS (Photograph: Stork Advisory Bureau)

Apple Cream Torte

METRIC/IMPERIAL

225 g/8 oz shortcrust pastry
750 g/1½ lb cooking apples, peeled, cored and sliced
50 g/2 oz butter or margarine
1 × 142 ml/¼ pint carton soured cream
50 g/2 oz plain flour
grated rind and juice of 1 lemon
100 g/4 oz granulated sugar
3 eggs, separated

Topping:
25 g/1 oz caster sugar
1 teaspoon cinnamon
50 g/2 oz dried breadcrumbs
25 g/1 oz flaked almonds

AMERICAN

½ lb basic pie dough, made with all-purpose flour
1½ lb baking apples, peeled, cored and sliced
¼ cup butter or margarine
⅔ cup sour cream
¼ cup all-purpose flour
grated rind and juice of 1 lemon
½ cup sugar
3 eggs separated

Topping:
2 tablespoons sugar
1 teaspoon cinnamon
½ cup dried bread crumbs
¼ cup slivered almonds

Line a swiss roll tin (jelly roll pan) 18 cm × 25.5 cm (7 in × 10 in) with pastry. Prick base and bake blind in a moderately hot oven (200°C/400°F, Gas Mark 6).

Fry the apple slices in the butter over a low heat until tender, stirring frequently.

Blend together the soured (sour) cream, flour, lemon rind and juice, sugar and egg yolks and pour over the apples. Stir over a low heat until the mixture thickens.

Whisk egg whites until stiff and fold into the apple mixture. Pour into the pastry case.

Mix topping ingredients and sprinkle over the surface. Bake in a preheated moderate oven (180°C/350°F, Gas Mark 4) for about 30 minutes until set.

Serve hot or cold with whipped cream.

Serves 8

PRESERVES

Apricot Jam

METRIC/IMPERIAL
1.75 kg/4 lb fresh apricots
450 ml/¾ pint water
3 tablespoons lemon juice
1.75 kg/4 lb sugar

AMERICAN
4 lb fresh apricots
2 cups water
3 tablespoons lemon juice
8 cups sugar

Wash, halve and stone the apricots. Crack a few stones and remove the kernels; blanch in boiling water for 2 minutes.

Put the apricots into a pan with the water, lemon juice and blanched kernels. Simmer until the fruit is soft and the contents of the pan well reduced. Add the sugar, stir until dissolved, then boil rapidly for about 15 minutes, or until setting point is reached. Pot and cover in the usual way.

Makes about 3 kg/6½ lb

Strawberry Jam

METRIC/IMPERIAL
1.5 kg/3½ lb small strawberries
3 tablespoons lemon juice
1.5 kg/3 lb sugar

AMERICAN
3½ lb small strawberries
3 tablespoons lemon juice
6 cups sugar

Hull and wash the strawberries, put into a pan with the lemon juice and simmer gently, without adding water, for 25 minutes until soft but not mushy. Add the sugar, stir until dissolved, then boil rapidly until setting point is reached.

Allow to cool for about 20 minutes, to prevent the fruit rising in the jars, then pot and cover in the usual way.

Makes about 2.25 kg/5 lb

Bottling:

Bottling may not be everyone's favourite method of preserving but if you do not own a freezer – and do have plenty of cool, dark storage space – it is well worth devoting the time to storing fruit in this way, especially when there is a glut. Although you have to buy special preserving jars, these can be used over and over again, with new sealing rings.

The fruit must be fresh, sound, free of disease, clean and properly ripe – neither too soft, nor too hard. Choose fruits of a similar shape, size and ripeness for any one bottle.

Cherries in Syrup

Whole cherries: remove stalks and wash. Stoned cherries: use a cherry stoner or small knife to remove the stones. Collect any juice and include with the fruit, if liked.

Add 1 teaspoon citric acid to each $4\frac{1}{2}$ litres/1 gallon of syrup (with either black or white cherries) to improve the colour and flavour.

Apricots in Syrup

Whole apricots: remove stalks, wash fruit. Halved apricots: make a cut round each fruit up to the stone, twist the two halves apart and remove the stone. Crack some stones to obtain the kernels and include with the fruit. Pack quickly into jars to prevent browning.

Bottling Method

Use special bottling jars with glass caps or metal discs secured by screw-bands or clips. If the cap or disc has no fitted rubber gasket, thick rubber rings are inserted between it and the top of the jar. Neither the rubber rings, nor the metal discs with fitted seals should be used more than once.

Before use, check jars and fittings for any flaw and test to make sure they are air-tight. To do this, fill with water, putting fittings in place, then turn upside down. Any leak will show in 10 minutes.

Jars must be absolutely clean, so wash them and rinse in clean hot water.

You can use either water or syrup, but syrup gives a better flavour and colour. The usual proportion is 225 g/8 oz/1 cup sugar to 600 ml/1 pint/$2\frac{1}{2}$ cups water, but the amount varies according to the sweetness of the fruit.

Use granulated sugar; dissolve in half the required amount of water; bring to the boil for 1 minute. Then add the remainder of the water. This method reduces the time needed for the syrup to cool.

Put the fruit in the jars, layer by layer, using a packing spoon or the handle of a wooden spoon. When the jar is full, the fruit should be firmly and securely wedged in place, without bruising or squashing. The more closely the fruit is packed, the less likely it is to rise after the shrinkage which may occur during processing.

Heat the oven to cool (150°C/300°F, Gas Mark 2). Fill the packed jars with

APRICOT JAM, STRAWBERRY JAM *(page 83)*, CHERRIES IN SYRUP, APRICOTS IN SYRUP *(page 84) (Photograph: British Sugar Bureau)*

boiling syrup or water to within 2.5 cm/1 in of the top. Put on rubber rings, glass caps or metal discs, but not the screw bands or clips. Place the jars 5 cm/2 in apart on a solid baking sheet lined with newspaper to catch any liquid which may boil over. Put in the centre of the oven, allowing 40 to 50 minutes for every $\frac{1}{2}$ to 1.75 kg/1 to 4 lb in the oven.

Remove the jars one by one and put on clips or screw bands – screwing the bands as tightly as possible. Allow to become quite cold.

Lemon and Whisky Marmalade

METRIC/IMPERIAL
750 g/1½ lb lemons
1.5 litres/2½ pints water
1.5 kg/3 lb sugar
1 miniature bottle whisky

AMERICAN
1½ lb lemons
6¼ cups water
6 cups sugar
1 miniature bottle whisky

Scrub the lemons, cut in half, squeeze out the juice and reserve the pips. Cut the peel into thin strips. Put the peel and juice into a large pan with the water. Tie the pips in a muslin bag and add to the pan. Cook gently for about 1½ hours or until the peel is soft.

Remove the bag of pips and stir in the sugar. Stir until the sugar has dissolved, then boil quickly until setting point is reached.

Remove any scum, then stir in the whisky. Allow to cool for about 30 minutes, then pour into sterilized jars. Seal and label.
Makes about 2.25 kg/5 lb

Lime Marmalade

METRIC/IMPERIAL
750 g/1½ lb limes
1.5 litres/2½ pints water
1.5 kg/3 lb sugar

AMERICAN
1½ lb limes
6¼ cups water
6 cups sugar

Scrub fruit, cut in half, squeeze out the juice and reserve the pips. Cut the peel into thin strips. Put the peel and juice into a large pan with the water. Tie the pips in a muslin bag and add to the pan. Cook gently for about 1½ hours, or until the peel is soft.

Remove the bag of pips and stir in the sugar. Stir until the sugar has dissolved, then boil rapidly until setting point is reached.

Remove any scum and leave to cool for 30 minutes. Pour into sterilized jars, seal and label.
Makes about 2.25 kg/5 lb

Cider and Orange Marmalade

METRIC/IMPERIAL	AMERICAN
750 g/1½ lb Seville oranges	1½ lb Seville oranges
juice of 2 lemons	juice of 2 lemons
1.5 litres/2½ pints dry cider	6¼ cups dry hard cider
600 ml/1 pint water	2½ cups water
1.5 kg/3 lb sugar	6 cups sugar

Scrub the oranges, cut in half, squeeze out the juice, reserving the pips, and cut the peel into thin strips. Put the peel, orange and lemon juice into a large pan with the cider and water. Tie the pips in a muslin bag and add to the pan. Cook gently for about 1½ hours or until the peel is soft.

Remove the bag of pips and stir in the sugar. Stir until the sugar has dissolved. Boil rapidly until setting point is reached.

Remove any scum. Allow to cool for 30 minutes. Pour into sterilized jars, seal and label.

Makes about 2.25 kg/5 lb

Grapefruit Jelly

METRIC/IMPERIAL	AMERICAN
3 grapefruit	3 grapefruit
4 lemons	4 lemons
2.25 litres/4 pints water	10 cups water
1.5 kg/3 lb sugar	6 cups sugar

Scrub the fruit, then roughly chop and place it into a pan with the water. Bring to the boil, cover and simmer gently for about 2 hours, or until peel is soft.

Strain through muslin, squeezing all the juice out of the bag. Return the juice to the pan and stir in the sugar. Stir until sugar has dissolved.

Boil rapidly until setting point is reached. Remove any scum, then pour quickly into sterilized jars, seal and label. Do not tilt jars before jelly has set.

Makes about 2.25 kg/5 lb

Pickled Pears

METRIC/IMPERIAL
1 kg/2 lb firm eating pears
boiling water to cover
450 ml/¾ pint cider vinegar
300 ml/½ pint water
500 g/1 lb sugar
1 cinnamon stick
10 whole cloves
small piece of root ginger

AMERICAN
2 lb firm eating pears
boiling water to cover
2 cups cider vinegar
1¼ cups water
2 cups sugar
1 cinnamon stick
10 whole cloves
small piece of root ginger

Peel, core and quarter the pears. Put them in a pan and cover with boiling water. Cook gently for 10 minutes until just tender. Drain. Boil the remaining ingredients together for 5 minutes then add the pears. Cook until the pears are transparent.

Drain the pears, pack into sterilized jars and cover with boiling syrup. Seal and store in a cool dark place for at least a month before eating.
Makes about 1.5 kg/3 lb

Sweet and Sour Onions

METRIC/IMPERIAL
1 kg/2 lb pickling onions
225 g/8 oz salt
2.25 litres/4 pints water
225 g/8 oz demerara sugar
600 ml/1 pint malt vinegar
1 tablespoon pickling spice

AMERICAN
2 lb pickling onions
⅔ cup salt
10 cups water
1¼ cups brown sugar
2½ cups malt vinegar
1 tablespoon pickling spice

Place the onions in a large saucepan with the salt and water, stir until the salt dissolves. Put a plate on top to keep the onions under the brine and leave for 12 hours.

Peel the onions and return to the brine for a further 24 hours.

Meanwhile, make up the spiced vinegar. Dissolve the sugar in the vinegar over a low heat, stir in the spice, bring slowly to the boil and boil for ½ a minute. Leave to cool.

Drain the onions well, and pack into sterilized jars. Strain the vinegar and pour over the onions. Seal and store for 3 to 4 months to mature before eating.
Makes about 1.5 kg/3 lb

APPLE MINT BUTTER *(page 90)*, PICKLED PEARS, SWEET AND SOUR ONIONS *(page 88)*, TOMATO JAM *(page 90)* *(Photograph: British Sugar Bureau)*

88

PICKLED PEARS

APPLE MINT BUTTER

SWEET AND SOUR ONIONS

TOMATO JAM

Apple Mint Butter

METRIC/IMPERIAL
1.5 kg/3 lb cooking apples
600 ml/1 pint water
1.5 kg/3 lb sugar
3 tablespoons lemon juice
1 tablespoon malt vinegar
50 g/2 oz chopped fresh mint

AMERICAN
3 lb baking apples
$2\frac{1}{2}$ cups water
6 cups sugar
3 tablespoons lemon juice
1 tablespoon malt vinegar
$1\frac{1}{2}$ cups chopped fresh mint

Prepare and slice the apples into a large saucepan, add the water, cover and cook gently until the apples become pulpy. Stir in the sugar until dissolved. Add the lemon juice, bring to the boil and boil rapidly, stirring frequently to prevent the mixture from burning.

Cook until thick. Remove pan from the heat and test by dripping a little of the mixture on a saucer. Allow to cool. If, on cooling, it forms a skin which wrinkles when pressed, it is sufficiently cooked. Stir in the vinegar and chopped mint. Pour into sterilized jars, seal and label.

Makes about 2.25 kg/5 lb

Tomato jam

METRIC/IMPERIAL
1 kg/$2\frac{1}{4}$ lb firm tomatoes
1 kg/$2\frac{1}{4}$ lb granulated sugar
4 tablespoons lemon juice

AMERICAN
$2\frac{1}{4}$ lb firm tomatoes
$4\frac{1}{2}$ cups sugar
4 tablespoons lemon juice

Skin tomatoes, cut into quarters, place in a saucepan, cover with sugar and leave to stand overnight. The following day, gently heat, stirring, to dissolve the sugar, add the lemon juice and boil the jam fast until setting point is reached.

Allow the jam to stand for 5 minutes before pouring into warm jars. Seal with waxed discs. When cool, cover, seal and label.

Makes about 2 kg/$4\frac{1}{2}$ lb

INDEX

INDEX

The editor would like to thank the following for their assistance in compiling this book:-

The African Groundnut Council; The Apple and Pear Development Council; Blue Band Bureau; British Egg Information Service; British Bacon Bureau; British Sugar Bureau; British Turkey Federation; Buxted Advisory Bureau; The Cadbury Typhoo Food Advisory Service; Cheeses From Switzerland Ltd; Colman Foods; The Danish Centre, London; The Dutch Fruit and Vegetable Bureau; Frank Cooper; Fyffes Group; Haywards Pickles; John West Foods; Kellogg's Kitchen; Knorr Soups; Marmite; Mars Health Education Fund; Michegan Baked Bean Kitchen; Milk Marketing Board; Mushrooms Growers' Association; The New Zealand Lamb Information Bureau; The Oxo Meal Planning Service; Outline Slimming Bureau; Potato Marketing Board; Stork Cookery Service; Tate & Lyle Test Kitchen; Taunton Cider; Tupperware